ahead of i

Clocktower Press published its first booklet, featuring stories by James Meek and Duncan McLean, in 1990. Over the next six years, further booklets gave space to early work by unknown writers like Irvine Welsh and Alan Warner, as well as new fiction by more established names such as Janice Galloway and James Kelman. There are no plans to produce any more Clocktower booklets, but this anthology contains exciting work by writers new to Clocktower, as well as a generous selection from past publications – all of which are now out of print, and almost as hard to get hold of as some of the authors Clocktower championed.

also by Duncan McLean

BUCKET OF TONGUES
BLACKDEN
BUNKER MAN
LONE STAR SWING

ahead of
its time

a Clocktower Press anthology

edited by
Duncan McLean

JONATHAN CAPE
LONDON

First published 1997

1 3 5 7 9 10 8 6 4 2

This selection and introduction © Duncan McLean 1997

Individual pieces © each author

Duncan McLean has asserted his right
under the Copyright, Designs and Patents Act 1988
to be identified as the author of this work

First published in the United Kingdom in 1997 by Jonathan Cape,
Random House, 20 Vauxhall Bridge Road, London SW1V 2SA

Random House Australia (Pty) Limited
20 Alfred Street, Milsons Point, Sydney,
New South Wales 2061, Australia

Random House New Zealand Limited
18 Poland Road, Glenfield,
Auckland 10, New Zealand

Random House South Africa (Pty) Limited
Endulini, 5A Jubilee Road,
Parktown 2193, South Africa

Random House UK Limited Reg. No. 954009

Clocktower logo by Eddie Farrell

A CIP catalogue record for this book is available from the British Library

Papers used by Random House UK Limited are natural,
recyclable products made from wood grown in sustainable forests.
The manufacturing processes conform to the environmental
regulations of the country of origin.

ISBN 0–224–05024–9

Typeset by Palimpsest Book Production Limited,
Polmont, Stirlingshire
Printed and bound in Great Britain
by Mackays of Chatham PLC

contents

II

TIME BOMBS

A short history of the Clocktower Press

By the autumn of 1990, I had been janitor of the village hall in South Queensferry, about ten miles west of Edinburgh, for two and a half years. During that time, I'd been trying to write fiction. For the first year or so my writing was dead on the page, but I persevered, trying different approaches, different angles of attack. Eventually I found a voice for the narrative – *my* voice, I suppose – and the stories came flooding out. I wasn't sure if they were any good or not, but I knew that they felt *alive* to me: scenes and characters fought their way off the page and into my mind. (*Out* of my mind and *onto* the page, surely? you say. Well, it didn't feel like that at the time: once I'd found the voice, the stories more or less told themselves. I just sat back and waited to see what these unpredictable, charged-up characters would say and do next.)

I wanted to share the stories with other folk: with readers. At the time, my friend James Meek (reporter for *The Scotsman* in those days) was about the only person interested in what I was trying to do. We'd meet up and swap typescripts, ideas and criticism. We'd even read our stories out loud to each other. But an audience of one wasn't enough for either of us.

Here's the crux: when James and I sent out our new stories to magazines across the land, they weren't all rejected out of hand. No, sometimes we got back constructive rejection slips. Very occasionally we even got letters of acceptance, from *Edinburgh Review, Iron, West Coast Magazine*. That was where the problems really came to a head. I mean, every writer expects rejection.

What you don't know to expect when you're starting out is the interminable wait from acceptance to publication. Magazines would take three or four months to tell us they'd been excited by our work and would like to publish it; and then there'd be a gap of at least six months – and often eighteen months or two *years* – before the stories actually appeared in print.

This was frustrating, as we were both trying to write new stories, written in the language of the day, about the ideas and problems that confronted us here and now. Ezra Pound said that literature is news that stays news. Commentators tend to focus on the notion of permanence in that statement, but it seems to me that the 'news' part is at least as important. Good writing should have a special impact if read the day or the week after it's written. Not that it can't still have an impact ten years or ten centuries later. But if it doesn't hit home when the ink's still wet, why should it when the paper's yellowed?

James and I decided we couldn't wait for the overworked, underpowered magazines to publish us. We'd do it ourselves. Taking inspiration from music and football fanzines, we decided that glossy production and distribution in prestigious outlets was less important that just getting our voices heard. So James typed out his latest story – 'Safe' – and mine – 'Lurch' – on his work computer, I took them to a photocopy shop in George Street, and 24 hours and £150 later, we had 300 copies of the first Clocktower booklet. James and I each put in fifty quid, by the way, with the third fifty coming from our friend, artist Eddie Farrell, who also provided the cover, and a logo based on the most prominent feature of the hall I looked after.

The response to *Safe/Lurch* was minimal. How could it have been anything else? We made little attempt to get press coverage, and none to persuade bookshops to sell the thing. What we did was post copies to twenty or thirty writers we respected and thought might enjoy it, give a few dozen to friends and relatives, sell handfuls at the very occasional readings we were starting to get asked to do. And immediately begin producing another one.

Vanity publishing? No doubt we *were* caught up in the excitement of seeing our work in print. And no doubt that was one of the reasons why we – and soon I by myself, as Eddie concentrated on his own art, and James's work took him to Kiev and Moscow – forged on with Clocktower. Certainly it was a great feeling to write a story one week, and, with only a small amount of time, expertise and money, be able to send it out into the world the next in a neatly stapled card cover. But mostly it was because I'd come to a realisation that this was what publishing was really all about: not a commercial, money-making venture, but a cultural intervention.

The booklets were intended to be literary time-bombs. At first glance they looked slight and inoffensive, even lightweight, but once they were out in the world, once the stories and poems they contained lodged in readers' minds, they'd start a chain reaction that would have disproportionately large effects.

A list of the booklets produced appears after these few words. The dates of publication underline that I never attempted to publish with any regularity; I always waited till I came across new work that really grabbed me, that *demanded* to be published, before committing all that money to Rank Xerox. As it happened, I never had to wait long.

A group of writers in Glasgow – Alasdair Gray and James Kelman in prose, Tom Leonard and Liz Lochhead in poetry – had risen to prominence in the early and mid eighties (their breakthrough books being respectively *Lanark* (1981), *Not Not While The Giro* (1983), *Intimate Voices* (1984) and *Dreaming Frankenstein* (1984)). The Glasgow writers were resolutely not a 'school', but as I understood it they did have at least one important thing in common: a commitment to the *voice* as the basis of literary art, rather than some supposed canonical 'officially approved' language. It didn't matter whether the official language was the RP of the dominant political and cultural establishments in London, or the Lallans of the Scots Style Sheet squad in Edinburgh; the Glasgow writers rejected the 'standards' and wrote in their own language.

They didn't invent this idea, of course. It's a tradition. It goes back at least as far as Dante and his decision to write in Tuscan rather than Latin. Chaucer's part of it. The work of all the great English Jacobean writers is rooted in everyday language. In the United States Whitman struggled to find an American voice, and succeeded; his achievements were built on by poets like William Carlos Williams, Louis Zukovsky and Charles Reznikoff (who in turn influenced the Glasgow writers). Back in Britain, the best bits of Scott and Dickens show their awareness of the tradition, and their worst bits show them straying away from it.

All around the world, writers have struggled to assert the right to write in their own language – often in the face of opposition from state policemen of one sort or another with a vested interest in keeping *their* language as the one of authority and power. The struggle goes on today: in the Arab countries, for instance, where there's a fierce, century-old debate over the relative merits of *amiyya* (the spoken language) and *fusha* (literary Arabic). And in 1995, Ken Saro-Wiwa, author of, amongst other things, *Sozaboy: A novel in rotten English*, was hanged by state authorities in Nigeria. 'This language is disordered and disorderly,' Saro-Wiwa wrote in an introductory note to the novel. 'It thrives on lawlessness, and is part of the dislocated and discordant society in which Sozaboy must live.'

The Glasgow writers introduced or reintroduced such ideas to Britain. Barring a very few individuals who'd made themselves exceptions – Tony Harrison in England, for instance, Edwin Morgan and Ian Hamilton Finlay in Scotland, all poets – the tradition seemed to have died out, or at least disappeared from view.

Fiction as a serious, searching medium seemed to be on the point of dying out too. The best England could offer was pastiches of Victorian novels (harking back to a time when writers still had access to living language) and cobbled-together patchworks of half-grasped argots, ad-talk, and transatlantic idioms (they lurched and creaked like Frankenstein's monster fake-languages, but never really came to life).

By the late eighties, however, readers all over Scotland had caught up with what the Glasgow writers were doing, and the importance of it. Some of those readers were writers themselves. Many of them went off and started the search for their own voices, the voices that might tell the stories of the places they came from. For the great effect the Glasgow writers had was not to inspire people across the land to start writing in Glaswegian. No, the effect was to send folk off to listen to themselves – and to their families, friends and workmates – and start from there.

James Meek and I were doing that in 'Safe' and 'Lurch'. What we found shortly after publishing those stories was that there were dozens of writers – usually solitary, sometimes lucky enough to have come across a kindred-spirit or two – doing the same thing throughout the country. By various circuitous routes they found the early Clocktower booklets, and wrote to order more, to offer support and encouragement, to submit their own work. And gradually Clocktower started to publish writers such as Gordon Legge, David Millar and Jim Ferguson. 'Time For A Change' was the motto on our first title-page, and it really did start to feel like things were moving. Other underground publishers were springing up too: Ferguson and Bobby Christie ran the Neruda Press in Glasgow, and Edinburgh had Ramsey Kanaan's AK Press and, slightly later, Rebel Inc.

In 1991, I was asked to run a writers' group in Muirhouse, in north Edinburgh. There were well-attended readings featuring such folk as Ferguson, Legge, Kelman and Janet Paisley, and opportunities for local writers to read and discuss their work. One of these local writers was Kevin Williamson, who brought poems, stories and boundless energy to the group; a year or so later he started *Rebel Inc.* magazine. Another was Alison Kermack, a poet who blended Tom Leonard and Ntozake Shange and came up with something entirely her own; her booklet was one of Clocktower's fastest sellers.

Our slowest seller was undoubtedly *Past Tense: four stories from a novel*, by Irvine Welsh (the novel being *Trainspotting*). Welsh had grown up in Muirhouse, but was living in Leith by this time. His debut publication – 'First Day Of The Edinburgh Festival' – was in *New Writing Scotland 9*, edited by Janice Galloway and Hamish Whyte and published in October 1991. I liked that story a lot and asked Janice what she knew about its author: nothing. 'Irvine Welsh is currently completing a brightly optimistic novel full of sympathetic, generously spirited characters,' said his biographical note in *NWS*. Eventually I tracked him down, we met a few times, and in April 1992 Clocktower published *Past Tense*, with powerful illustrations by Peter Govan. In those days, to write about heroin addicts on a run-down Edinburgh estate was far from the easy commercialism cynical critics often accuse Irvine of having adopted. Quite the opposite: only a few folk shared my enthusiasm for what he was doing. Luckily, one of those few was Kevin Williamson. When the first issue of *Rebel Inc.* came out on 1 May, it had another great piece by Irvine in it, as well as work by Alison Kermack, Gordon Legge and me, amongst others. Kevin's commitment to the new writing that was starting to break out all over the east coast, combined with his talent for promotion, publicity and distribution, meant that *Rebel Inc.* had an enormous impact: people all over the country, and in all the media, were talking about a literary magazine – a rare occurrence!

Gordon Legge used to cycle along from his home in Grangemouth to visit the hall in South Queensferry; we would spend hours discussing books, records, and the (mis)fortunes of Falkirk FC. After I moved to Orkney, Gordon decided he would like to have more of those discussions, so in the summer of '93 he travelled two hundred miles northwards . . . on his trusty pusher. While he was there, I remember I gave him some manuscripts I'd received, unsolicited. They'd come from an Oban-born, Edinburgh-based train driver by the name of Alan Warner. Gordon agreed that they were funny and weird and original, and before long another name was added to the Clocktower roster.

The first booklet to be published from Orkney was *Parcel Of Rogues*. The idea for this one came from another Edinburgh writer (and Trocchi expert) David Millar. David had planned to start a magazine of that name, and had gathered together some good work from mostly unknown contributors. I had helped out by contacting a few more established writers and soliciting contributions from them. As it happened, the magazine ran into funding difficulties (and anyway, *Rebel Inc.* had cornered the market by this time . . .) so I suggested we issue the stuff we'd collected as a Clocktower booklet. At fifty-six pages, this has been Clocktower's biggest production to date. It is also, arguably, the most distinguished: as well as excerpts from *Trainspotting* and Janice Galloway's acclaimed *Foreign Parts*, it included the opening of an as-yet-untitled novel by James Kelman. A couple of years later, the novel was published as *How Late It Was, How Late*, and won the Booker Prize.

Clocktower has always been about seeking out the new, the exploratory, the unsafe. All three adjectives fit the work of Brent Hodgson, one of the most original and protean of modern Scottish writers. It's probably the impossibility of pigeon-holing Brent's writing that has left it uncollected by a major publisher so far, but his unique mix of humour and formal experiment (somewhere between Ivor Cutler and Ian Hamilton Finlay) has a growing following.

The same could be said of John Aberdein. His funny, acidic, sexy stories, composed in a fairly dense phonetic rendering of Aberdeen speech, are bold (and, I think, successful) experiments in pushing back the boundaries of Scots narrative. A few years ago, it could have been safely predicted that no more than a handful of dedicated Scottish readers would bother to look at such stuff, but the worldwide success of Irvine Welsh's almost-as-dense Leith-speak proves that hundreds of thousands of people are now prepared to stretch their minds to take in Scottish vocabulary, orthography and phonetics. Explorations in these areas can be seen on just about every page of this book, and the variety of approaches taken is very exciting.

There isn't space here to enumerate the qualities of every writer that's appeared in Clocktower. Neither is there space, unfortunately, to reprint all their work in this anthology. Some of the writing that first appeared in Clocktower is so widely available now that it would be daft to reprint it again anyway. For, as well as a celebration of Clocktower's past, and a reminder of where and how some of the current Scottish writers got their start, *Ahead Of Its Time* aspires to be just that. Of the new material which makes up the second half of the book, some is the current work of past Clocktower contributors, and some is by authors I've wanted to feature in Clocktower for some time but have never managed to till now.

They are evidence, if it is needed, that the current surge of good Scottish writing is much wider and deeper than allowed by the central-belt-squalor stereotype so beloved of Tartan Tories and middle-brow newspaper pundits. Ali Smith was born in Inverness, Leila Aboulela in Khartoum; Shug Hanlon comes from Falkirk; Robert Alan Jamieson is a Shetlander who lived for several years just outside South Queensferry, where he was a keen supporter of Clocktower's early efforts. Their work – and the ongoing work of all Clocktower's contributors, whether represented here or not – proves one thing beyond doubt: it's a good time to be alive and reading.

Duncan McLean
Orkney, March 1997

CLOCKTOWER PRESS
A Bibliography

There were ten Clocktower booklets, as follows. All consisted of short stories (sometimes *very* short) except where indicated. Pieces are listed in the order they appeared in the booklets.

1. *Safe/Lurch*
'Safe' by James Meek, subsequently included in *Last Orders* (Polygon, 1992) and 'Lurch' by Duncan McLean, subsequently included in *Bucket of Tongues* (Secker & Warburg, 1992). Cover by Eddie Farrell, graphics by Olivia Irvine.
16 pages, edition of 300.
Motto: *Time For A Change.*
Published December 1990 in South Queensferry.

2. *The Druids Shite It, Fail To Show*
'The Druids Shite It, Faii To Show' by Duncan McLean, later altered and included in *Bucket of Tongues*.
Cover and graphics by Jane Hyslop.
20 pages, edition of 300.
Motto: *Time For A Change.*
Published March 1991 in South Queensferry.

3. *Zoomers: short sharp fiction*
'Neighbours', 'Clumsy', 'Shame', 'Our Donna', 'Upon Meeting Janice Hetherston', 'First Day At Work', 'Life On A Scottish Council Estate Vol 2 Chap 1', 'The Joy of Knowledge'

and 'Life' by Gordon Legge. 'Someone Would Have To Go' and 'The Oxford Book Of Shopping And Fucking' by James Meek. 'Fair Play', 'Thistle Story' and 'The Big Man That Dropped Dead' by Duncan McLean, the latter two collected in *Bucket of Tongues*. 'An Impossible Gymnasium', 'Visiting Dignitary', 'Sex And Booze' and 'The Device' by Jim Ferguson. 'The Dictator And The Visitor In White' and 'Short Story' by Stefano Benni, translated from the Italian by Giacomo Mansueto. 'on the bridge tonight' by sandy watson.
Cover and graphics by Eddie Farrell.
20 pages, edition of 300.
Motto: *Time For A Quick One*.
Published July 1991 in South Queensferry.

4. *Restricted Vocabulary*
Poems by Alison Kermack: 'A Poyum', 'Process', 'iffyd gonty MA skule . . .', 'Non Sequitur', 'Thrown Out', 'The Perfect Soldier', 'Bemused', 'Houses', 'Dislekseeah', 'A Restricted Vocabulary', 'Culture Versus Convention'.
Cover and graphics by Alison Kermack.
16 pages, edition of 300.
Motto: *Time To Talk*.
Published November 1991 in South Queensferry.

5. *Past Tense: four stories from a novel*
Fiction by Irvine Welsh: 'Her Man', 'After The Burning', 'The Elusive Mr Hunt' and 'Winter In West Granton'. Later included in *Trainspotting* (Secker & Warburg, 1993).
Cover and graphics by Peter Govan.
16 pages, edition of 300.
Motto: *Time To Get Moving*.
Published April 1992 in South Queensferry.

6. *Parcel Of Rogues*
'Extract From A Novel In Progress' by Janice Galloway, later included in *Foreign Parts* (Jonathan Cape, 1994). 'Leavetaking', by Mary Kalugerovich. 'Untitled – From A Novel In Progress' by James Kelman, later rewritten as the start of *How Late It Was, How Late* (Secker & Warburg, 1994). '10 Shorts' by Gordon Legge. 'Why Doesn't He Talk To Me?' by David Millar. 'No Reservations' by Iain Mills. 'Homecoming' by Janet Paisley, later included in *Wildfire* (Taranis Books, 1992). 'Walter Mitty Slept Here' by Iain Walker. 'Recreation Time' by Billy Watt. 'Trainspotting At Leith Central Station', by Irvine Welsh, later included in *Trainspotting*.
Cover by Jane Hyslop, graphics by Eddie Farrell, Peter Govan and Alison Kermack.
56 pages, edition of 500 (some later lost in a flood).
Motto: *Time To Wrap Up*.
Published June 1992 in Stromness, Orkney.

7. *Collected Works: three novels, two lessons, nine haikus and more*
Poetry and prose by Brent Hodgson: 'It's Tough In The Tourist Industry', 'English Philosopher 1992', 'A Lesson', '*from* West of Scotland "Modern" Haikus', 'A Cheap Sleazy Glasga Porno Novel', '*from* West Of Scotland Haikus', 'Twa Fu Freens Frae Ayr: a novel', 'Green Bottles', 'Cabaret Programme For 1993 Season In The Auld Howff', 'Newly Wed: a Calvinistic novel for god-fearing clean-living Glaswegians', 'Another Lesson'.
Cover and graphics by Andrew Parkinson.
16 pages, edition of 300.
Motto: *Time Is A Word*.
Published October 1992 in Stromness, Orkney.

8. *Folk: more zoomers*
'Yonder Cunt', 'Blood Of Eden', 'A Spot Of Night Fishing', 'Smears 1 & 2' and 'A Good Impression' by Alan Warner. 'cracks', 'finished, and '*from* NO OTHER PLACE THAN WHERE I AM': poems by Jim Ferguson. 'Feerd', 'Uniform Feelings', 'Revolution' and 'Freedom Of Choice': poems by Alison Kermack. 'The Cruel Bastard And The Selfish Fucker Get It On', 'Robert K. Laird: Asexual History', 'Lots Of Laughter And Sex' and 'A Good Son' by Irvine Welsh, later collected as 'Sexual Disaster Quartet' in *Acid House* (Jonathan Cape, 1994). 'Some Kind Of Holy Holy', 'A Night Out', 'Fat Of The Land', 'Now, You're Staying With Your Auntie Jenny For A Week', 'Rival' and 'Suggestion': poems by Gordon Legge.
Cover and graphics by Caroline Hunter.
20 pages, edition of 300.
Motto: *Time Bombs*.
Published August 1993 in Stromness, Orkney.

9. *The Beetle House*
Poems by David Crystal: 'Skin Deep', 'A Beautiful Day', 'What He Told The Parkkeeper's Assistant', 'Strange Or Not', 'Only You Would Put An Empty Bottle In The Fridge', 'The Beetle House', 'Breakfast In Provence', 'Pigs', 'Jarrow Elvis', 'When The Penny Drops', 'Citizen Horse', 'The Perfect Boiled Egg', 'Incident At The Car Boot Sale', 'Soho Horse', 'Lucinda And Her Strange Sister', 'Spring And', 'Exiles part two', 'Studio 18', 'Swallow', 'East: a triptych', 'Albert Salmon', 'Isolato', 'Cider Monkey Frank', 'Sleaze'.
Cover by Nigel Burch.
28 pages, edition of 300.
Motto: *Time And Motion*.
Published September 1994 in Stromness, Orkney.

10. *The Can-Can, Ken?: A Dose O Dorics*
Fiction by John Aberdein: 'Jamie o Twabuggers', 'Eddirs', 'University o life, like', 'Hard Cunt', 'Concrete. Poetry.', 'The Odd Fish', 'The Can-Can, ken?', 'The Warld or Buckie', 'Trystin'.
Cover by Duncan McLean.
20 pages, edition of 300.
Motto: *Ahead Of Its Time.*
Published March 1996 in Stromness, Orkney.

There was also one *Clocktower Card*, as follows:

Own Words by Duncan McLean.
One sided business card, edition of 25.
Produced February 1994, on vending machine in John Menzies, Edinburgh, with the assistance of Alan Warner.

Many people helped produce one or more of the Clocktower booklets. In some cases the help was financial, in others it involved lending computers, or giving advice, or even typing and laying out an entire booklet. In all cases the assistance was invaluable. I'd like to thank these generous folk now: Mark Meredith, Nick Fiddes, Tom Arah, Edinburgh District Arts Council, Kevin Williamson, Robert Alan Jamieson, Pilton Print Resource Centre, The Merry Mac Fun Co, The Image Factory, Bill Cowan, Hoy Telecottage, Heather Black and Alan Warner. Most of all, I owe thanks to the writers and artists who allowed me to include their work in Clocktower Press publications, all for no cash and precious little glory. I hope it's some reward to see the time bombs we planted starting to go off.

I

CLOCKTOWER PRESS

ahead of its time

JAMES MEEK

Safe

Standing at the bus stop, not far from the centre of town, Fergus decided that he just wasn't safe. How could he hope to keep getting away with it all? He had to leave, even if it meant going to the ends of the earth, and this was now possible. If the director didn't call him in today, it would be the next day, or next week, and in the meantime he wouldn't be able to lift a spoonful of soup to his mouth without shaking so much that he'd spill it. So many people had his numbers that there was no way he would be able to hide in this country. No island was remote enough and the law offered no protection. Even before the police got involved there was the council, the inland revenue, the gas people, the electricity people, the bank, the building society, the newsagent, the Reader's Digest, the Automobile Association, the doctor, the dentist, the department of social security, the credit card companies. He just wasn't safe. It could all come crashing round his ears at any moment, and then what would he do? There would be nowhere to go and nobody would bail him out. Even if they didn't catch up with him soon the fear would destroy him. One way or another, everything he had could so easily be taken from him in a matter of moments. He just wasn't safe.

There was a travel agent across the road. In his wallet there was about £30 cash. He was on an overdraft of £150 but they might take a cheque for more than £50. The main thing was to be quick, they mustn't get a hold, otherwise he'd be even less safe with nothing to show for it. Access with about £300 on it and a £600 limit, Barclaycard with about £500 gone, £200 left, mind you they wouldn't let him use them both at once. But he could get a cash advance. If they didn't get clearance for any of the cards, he could buy the tickets with one, get an advance on the other, cash a cheque at another branch. Clothes. But that was it, if he made it, he would be safe, that kind of concern would just not be in the picture.

Excuse me, do you know if there's a travel agent round here? said Fergus to the man next to him.

Eh . . . the man looked round. I don't know. Is that one over there?

Fergus looked the way the man was pointing. Yes, he said, that's the one I spotted as well. It's cold, isn't it? He shivered and turned up his collar, and stamped his feet, grinning. His zip-up briefcase fell out from where he was gripping it, between his ribs and his elbow.

Whoops!

The man had taken several steps away from him. He was looking in a shop window. Nobody queued these days, they milled about the pavement and leaned in doorways, and when the bus came, it was just a rammy, being first in a queue of three and having five people pile on before any of you, it showed how completely unsafe things had become.

Fergus picked up the briefcase and wiped it clean with his sleeve. Watch your back. The bastards. He inspected the vinyl of the briefcase. It was marred. There was a scratch on it. He wept for a couple of moments. He blew his nose and wiped his eyes. You've got to protect your position. Safe.

He tapped the man on the shoulder. The man turned round, and started walking quickly away.

Cheerio! said Fergus. I'm not waiting for the bus, I'm going to that travel agent we both spotted together!

He pressed the crossing button. Immediately the lights

4

changed, the beeping started and the traffic stopped. Fergus crossed the road. Ha! He looked back; the traffic was still stopped. It was necessary to act very quickly. He squatted down and scraped the briefcase against the pavement. He straightened up. The amber lights were flashing. Not bad. The second scratch was a mirror image of the first, on the other side of the briefcase, at the opposite end. If there was to be another episode like this one, should he make four scratches, or let the situation change by only scratching it once, and then finally drop it, as if by accident? Good. If there was a place to scratch briefcases, or similar things, as a skill, for a living, as a gift. Come off it!

Come off it.

Can I help you, sir? said the woman in the travel agent's, one woman of five behind a counter, beside a computer terminal.

I'm looking for somewhere safe, said Fergus, sitting down in the chair opposite her. The chair had a very loose action, it was hard to resist the desire to swivel from side to side, he didn't want to annoy her, but it had a very loose action, maybe too loose in fact.

How d'you mean, said the woman.

Somewhere safe. Away. Abroad, said Fergus. They said Watch your back. I mean Christ, imagine saying a thing like that, eh.

You want to get away from it all.

Yeah, but it has to be safe.

Well, most of our European packages are ... there's no danger of disease in any of the resorts, you know. And crime's pretty low, you've got less chance of being mugged than here.

What parts of Europe?

Well, all the main holiday destinations.

I don't want a holiday, I want to go somewhere safe. Listen, I'm on a knife edge, you've got no idea. In the office, there's nowhere to hide, you're just totally exposed, and everyone knows where you live. Out there just now I managed to even things up, there was an incident with the briefcase, I kept my head and the balance is OK, but anything could happen later. This chair's a bit loose by the way, the swivel action. So it's got to be somewhere safe, I mean you must have hundreds of countries on your books, maybe I could just look through them, a few.

The woman gazed at him without saying anything, she turned away to the side. Why don't you just have a look through the brochures, she said.

I've got money.

Why don't you just have a look through the brochures, then we can have another talk about it. She smiled.

OK, only does it have to be you, if you're not free? I mean someone else might be seeing you, another customer, by that time.

You can see one of the other girls.

Then I won't have to sit on that chair, eh, cause it really is loose.

Right.

Fergus got up, crooking his briefcase under his elbow. He looked at the brochures. They seemed to be holidays mostly, they had an amazing number, but there was always the expectation you would come back. Also there was inevitably a beach and a hotel involved. They were sure to catch him out, he could be tracked down no bother and called back in no time. There were a couple of very thick brochures with stiff covers, they had trips to places like Moscow and Egypt and China. The cheapest one was £800 and after seven days you were finished, you just came back, totally out of touch for a week and coming back into the office, any safety you might have had you would just have given it all away in that time.

6

Have you got a map of the world? he asked the woman. She pointed.

Thanks. I mean I was really just wanting to have a look at the countries, there's bound to be one, isn't there.

The World, it said, Die Welt, Le Monde, Il Mondo, El Mundo, O Mundo. They weren't wrong when they said it was mostly water, what about all that blue. Antarctica, the Larsen Ice Shelf, sounded like a Scandinavian invention for keeping food fresh. Elephant Island, it didn't look like one, it'd be a reckless elephant set foot there among the penguins. Snow Island. Some imagination these geographers had. Drake Passage. Tight as a duck's. Dying of cold was altogether too safe.

There was no possibility of South America being safe, generals and conscripts and shanty towns, the jungles burning. It was a big place, though, all these cities he'd never heard of, maybe there was one the army missed and the Americans and the guerrillas, away from the insects and volcanoes and floods. Choele Choel, Huancavelica, Tonantins, Jacare-a-Canga, Barquisimeto. Three towns called Mercedes. A town called Sauce.

Hey! he shouted to the woman he had talked to. There's a town in Argentina called Sauce. Bet the taxi-drivers divide it up into Brown, Tomato —

Shit, he'd run out of sauces. What was the white one they served up with fish.

North America was out of the question. No one was safe in America, the numbers they had on you were staggering, and if you ran out of numbers, they would drop you like that and you'd die. Canada no way, anywhere with that woman's head on the currency was hardly to be trusted, they kept ties with the old country, distance meant nothing, they'd reach you with helicopters and seaplanes and snow buggies. Uranium City. That sounded so unsafe it could be a double bluff for the one safe place, but they still used the same money, they spoke the same language, it was the same authority. These parts of the world seemed to have been all coloured pink, making them easier to avoid, mind you so was Mongolia, they only had six colours plus blue for water.

Mongolia, now. It was too obvious. Running over the grasslands, waves of grassy ground to the horizon like the sea. They'd shrug their shoulders and send you away, what else could they do. There was a town called Moron. But then the Mongolian word for Moron was probably Aberdeen or something. Right now there was a Mongolian man in the travel agent's in Moron looking at a map of the world and considering Scotland, pink, the same colour, but much smaller, you could cover it with your thumb, Christ Genghis, I've never heard of these places, they must be safe. Dund-e-e. El-gin. Ooik.

Ooik.

Excuse me.

What? said Fergus.

Would you mind not talking to yourself? Otherwise I'll have to ask you to leave.

Sorry, said Fergus. I was just thinking about the Mongolian guy in Moron trying to pronounce Wick, you know. Sorry. It's this map, it's got Elgin and Wick but it doesn't have East Kilbride. Sorry.

The trouble was that he'd heard of all these countries, none of them had much of a safe ring, maybe he was being racist and believing what they said but China, Afghanistan, Iran, Korea, Cambodia, Vietnam, come on. And the office had branches all over the shop, for God's sake, Japan, Poland, Thailand, Turkey, Singapore, Taiwan, Israel. The trouble with Scandinavia was they were all so fucking rich. The trouble with Africa was they were all so fucking poor. That had a kind of safety in it maybe, but how could he join in? What would they think? A white man

8

in, eh, Yansanyama, they would think he was taking the piss. There were a few countries he hadn't heard of, but they were tiny wee places, and if he didn't know anything about them. All these islands in the South Pacific, they all had these great names only afterwards in brackets it told you who was calling the shots, France, Britain, USA.

The thing was to get to the place, and he'd get off the plane. They wouldn't have uniforms, they'd just be sitting or standing or having a meal when he arrived. They'd get up and wipe their mouths and take his luggage and his papers and all his clothes, the ones he was wearing as well, and put them back on the plane. They'd get together and find some new stuff for him to wear between them, and point down the road and say that's you, just keep going, all the best. And he'd go on, a quiet road, and people would pass and say hello. And he'd knock on a door and they'd say I'm sorry, dear, we've no room. And he'd try a few more doors and after a while they'd say, well, there's a spare room, you'll have to get a job and do your share of the chores around the house. And he'd say is there much work around here? They'd say there's always work to do. He'd say OK then. And they'd say come in, we'll be eating later.

Fergus sat down on the loose chair again.

Have you found something you like? said the woman.

To be totally honest with you, said Fergus, I'm a bit disappointed with the choice of countries.

That's a map of the world. That's all the countries there are.

I know, but I mean it just seems they've left something out. Fergus put his briefcase on the floor, gripped the seat of the chair with his hands and swivelled from side to side.

I don't really know what it is you want, said the woman, if you could give me a better idea.

I think, eh, I think it's just you'd arrive at the airport, get off the plane, and the people would be around, not with uniforms or anything, maybe having a meal or sweeping the place out, and they'd take all your papers and just throw them away, put them on the fire. Then you'd take off all your clothes.

Mr Sherman! The woman stood up and shouted into the back shop. Could you show this gentleman out, please!

There's no need to be rough, said Fergus, as Mr Sherman took him by the arm. Just let my fucking arm go, OK?

Come on, out you go, said Mr Sherman.

Was it the chair? said Fergus.

Get! said Mr Sherman.

I could try another one, said Fergus. He was on the street. He swung the briefcase in his hand. Coming out, now, he had left something behind, it always seemed safer inside than outside, some ways. He hadn't had much of a chance to explain the situation, he should have looked at the map for longer, Christ, he'd surely missed something. He could buy a book, but there wasn't time, he'd be late for work. Things were going very badly. He could fool them into thinking he was going to break the window. Well, he was going to. Yes.

Fergus threw his briefcase at the window of the travel agent's. It smacked against the centre of the glass which shuddered but didn't break. The briefcase flew on and skidded along the pavement. Fergus ran to pick it up.

Yeaah! he shouted. The scratch was right where he wanted it. He looked around and started walking alongside the nearest person, a woman wheeling a baby in a pushchair. It's OK, he said, they thought I was going to smash the window, so it was like I dropped the briefcase by accident, so the scratch is still valid, and I've got a deliberate scratch free now, there's still a space for one, it's just a boost for me until I can find another travel agent, I think I had something there in the line of me getting safe, but the seating was just abominable. Have you seen any travel agent's around?

Watch your back.

DUNCAN McLEAN

The Druids Shite It, Fail to Show

Colin was out in front, shouting the lead for the songs, clapping his hands, and the rest of the crew were behind him in a line across the road, chatting away, smoking, slagging each other off, and now and then joining in with Colin bawling, BOUNCY BOUNCY BOUNCY BOUNCY DYCE DYCE DYCE!

Back a bit, not bouncing or singing, sweating, Billy and Ray were following on, each of them lugging two massive carriers of cans. With every step, the bags of booze were banging against their legs.

We should've brought our fucking shinguards, said Billy.

A fucking car would've been more like the fucking business, said Ray.

Stop talking and start walking! somebody shouted from up ahead.

FUCK YOU! shouted back Billy.

Cammie stopped and turned, hands spread. Okay lads, point fucking taken, just keep the fucking pubes on. I'll tell you what, right, give us a can each and the bags won't be so heavy.

Like fuck we will! said Ray. You think we've carried it this fucking far to have you cunts get stuck in while our fucking hands are full!

Aye, no fucking chance Cam, said Billy, We're near enough there now, so you can just fucking wait and suffer like the rest of us.

Cammie was smiling: Well, I reckon you better just shut your fucking moaning then . . .

I reckon you better just fuck off, Billy came in. I mean it wasn't my fucking idea to come away up here. I've been up here afore with that mad bastard, I kent it was a bugger of a walk. If you're peched out from walking it's fucking Colin you should be complaining to.

Cammie grinned and laughed, and walked faster for a few seconds till he joined up with the lads ahead again, joined up with the bunch of them and joined in with the singing, HELLO HELLO WE ARE THE BEACH END BOYS!

I tell you what, said Ray, We should never've agreed to fucking tossing a coin for this fucking job.

Tossing a quine, said Billy, Now that would've been more acceptable.

Ray laughed. Nah, he said, I mean we should just've worked out a rota system, fucking taken it in turns man. Christ, these handles are cutting into my skin like blades!

They'd left the edge of town behind by this time and had been making their way up a farm track for a while, clouds of stew rising up under their trainers, drifting back into the eyes and mouths of Ray and Billy coming up in the rear. And the two of them were also stubbing over ruts and potholes in the road.

Is it much fucking further is it? said Ray, breathing hard.

No, look, said Billy, and nodded up ahead to where the crew had come to a stop at a gate by the side of the track.

As Ray and Billy caught up with them, Colin was lifting a circle of twine off the stoup. He nodded at them. Come in to the body of the kirk, he said, then, as the gate started to swing open, he jumped onto the bottom bar and swung with it, pointing into the park and shouting, CHARGE! Fifty yards away, at the top end of the park, there was a clump of trees raised up on a grassy knowe.

The lads looked at each other, then Pidge said, Eh, is that

all there is to it then? I mean where's the fucking mystic remains, eh?

What! said Colin, jumping down off the gate, Can you not feel strange forces in the air? Whoohoohoo!

Aye aye, Col's been on the magic mushers again, said Duggy.

Come on, let's get moving, said Colin. It's a mental place, that wee wood. Let's go! And he marched off across the dreels. There was a shrugging of shoulders, then folk started after him. Halfway across the park, Colin turned and shouted back, Don't forget the Country Code: shut the fucking gate!

Aye, better not let the sheep and that escape, said Beamer.

Right enough, you'll be needing them later on, said Cammie.

Everybody laughed, and then Pidge started singing, Sheep-shagging bastard, he's a sheep-shagging bastard! And everybody else started giving it laldie too, except Beamer, who was standing there going red in the face, and Billy, who had passed his bags of carry-out to Duggy and gone back to close the gate.

After a few minutes they were at the end of the park, and Colin climbed up onto the dyke surrounding the trees and turned back to face the crew, who were all shouting and laughing now, trying to nick cans from the carriers, looking up trying to make out what was on top of the mound amongst the trees. Colin threw his arms apart in a cutting movement, and when the noise only half-stopped, he shouted, Silent drill! Everyone shut up and looked at him, and he raised a finger to his lips, shushing them, then signalled with it for them to come up and over the dyke one by one. Cammie went first, then Pidge, Billy, Duggy handing the booze bags to Colin first, Ray next, doing the same, Beamer last, till they were all in over, and Colin louped down beside them. Through all this nobody opened their mouth to speak, and the sounds of the town were left far behind and below now; the only noises were the occasional clatter of an oil-rig chopper carried on the wind from the heliport a couple of miles away, and caw-coughing craws from some big black birds in the trees overhead.

Colin passed to the front of the crew and led them up the slope, through the trees and out into a slight dip in the ground which was followed by a clear grassy space with the big grey jagged stones ranged around its edges. Colin held up a hand, and the others stopped in the middle of the stone circle.

Lads, said Colin, These are the Devil Stanes . . .

None of the Dyce Casual Crew moved or spoke at all. They stood and looked round at the tall flat slabs, some of them even taller and broader than Duggy, rising straight out of the earth, others looking shorter, leaning at various angles, half tipped over by tree roots or something. A couple were completely couped and partly grown over with grass and red moss. The hoodies were keckling up above, the wind was guttering through holes in the dyke and branches, and the crew was in total silence.

SHITING IT LADS? shouted Colin suddenly and immediately everyone was talking and laughing and stepping from foot to foot, walking about the clearing. A couple folk took off their jackets, and Ray hung his shell-top over one of the stones.

Crack open the bevvy! called Duggy, and a cheer went up as the carriers were emptied out onto the short grass, near to where someone had had a fire going fairly recently.

I'm fucking parched by the way, said Pidge, and he grabbed at the can that Duggy had just opened.

Get your own you cunt, said Duggy, turning away. There's plenty for everyfuckingbody.

It is hot though, eh? said Beamer.

Hot enough to make you beam, said Ray. He put on a cheesy grin and slapped at his cheeks.

I reckon we should've gone down to the beach, said Beamer.

I'm fucking fed-up of the carnies, said Ray.

Aye, but I'm not talking about them, am I: I'm saying it's hot enough to get going in the water, ken.

A few folk laughed. Shite! shouted Cammie from the other side of the circle.

Feel this fucking heat man, Beamer went on. It would've been grand mucking about in the sea, and we could've got the bus straight there, instead of climbing all these fucking hills.

Cut the fucking peenging, said Colin. Christ, it was only one wee fucking hill we had to climb: if you're not fit for that . . . Jesus!

All the lads were looking at Beamer, who was starting to go even redder in the face. Colin spoke again:

Anyway, the sea won't be hot enough for swimming. It doesn't heat up, that's the problem with the bastarding sea around here, it just doesn't fucking heat up: no matter how hot the weather is, the water's still cold enough to freeze your chugs off. If you had any, you peenging fucking poofjuice!

Beamer took a big swallow of lager, then he said, Still, we could've given it a go. And if it was too nippy, we could've gone to the carnies as a last resort.

A few groans went up.

I just can't be arsed with that place, said Ray, shaking his head. I used to like the shows, but I'm just fucking . . . fed up of them these days.

Tell you what Beamer, said Colin. Next time we're down there, we'll go to that Test Your Fist machine and draw your face on the fucking punch ball.

Everybody laughed. Profits'll soar, said Pidge.

Aye, we'll get one of your old floppy hats and stick that on top, said Cammie. Nobody'll ken the difference! Big and round and red as fuck: is it the ball or is it Beamer's head?

I had to buy a new hat this week, said Beamer.

Ah-ha! Changing the fucking subject you cunt! said Cammie.

No, I did though, they only last about three fucking games, then they're so muckit you can just forget about them.

Aye, you're right enough, said Ray. He had taken off his hat and was twirling it round on one finger of his non-drinking hand. If you try and wash them they end up looking like shite, all frayed and white and that: the red just comes flooding out.

Blood! said Pidge.

You'd ken about that right enough Pidge, said Colin. Hey, Ray, Billy, you missed yourselves yesterday, you should've seen this cunt! Jesus, speak about blood . . .

What're you talking about? said Billy from the far side of the circle where he was sitting and drinking, leaning back on one of the big stones.

You could've made a black pudding out of Pidge's spillings yesterday, said Cammie.

Colin jumped up from behind his pile of cans, and started jumping about amongst the crew and their carry-out, dancing about in the middle of the circle.

It was fucking MAGIC man, I'm telling you! he said, stomping on the grass at Billy's feet. Me and Pidge and Cammie and Duggy, we came out of Tannadice, right – after our historic victory – and there was this massive fucking escort waiting, pigs on horses and everything. Right away! I thought, and we decided we'd give that the fucking swerve. There'd been no fun in the ground, ken, and we didn't fancy going straight back to the fucking station and home.

You could've got off at Arbroath or somewhere, said Billy.

Wise up, said Pidge. We're in the middle of fucking Castle Street Dundee, and you're talking about Arbroath! Smokie Soccer Crew versus Tayside Trendies? No competition man!

Colin cleared his throat, looked at Billy and Pidge, then went on, So we're outside this pub, Reflections or something, and there's fuck all going on, right, there's nobody in the town but a few old scarfers. And we were more or less going to call it a day – eh Cam? – when there was this roaring and cheering, and we looked around and there were about twenty of the fuckers, piling out the swing doors of this bar . . . half the cunts still with glasses in their hands!

So did you run for it?

We didn't have time to run! We didn't have time to fucking turn around! One minute I was thinking the day was a wipe-out, the next thing I kent I was on the floor with some jute bastard kicking my head in!

And see me? said Pidge, Well I was furthest away, so I made a break for it.

Fucking bottled it, said Cammie.

Too fucking right, said Pidge, Tactical retreat I'd call it.

I bet Duggy never ran, said Ray.

No way I never.

Duggy never runs, said Billy, He's no brains. Everybody laughed.

Aye, and you've no balls Billy-boy.

Stop fucking bargling and get on with the fucking story, said Beamer.

Me and Cammie were on the ground, said Colin, And Duggy as well, we were just fucking outnumbered, we'd no chance. So, they've been putting the boot into us for a while, and then they see Pidge bombing away down the road, and one of them shouts, After him, don't let him away!

They thought I was the leader.

Now there's a fucking joke, eh! Anyway, it was a magic laugh, the three of us were left behind, a bit worse for wear and tear but basically A-okay, so we get up, brush ourselves down . . .

Aye, you didn't rush to come and help me, did you?

We thought you'd got clean away, said Colin, turning away to wink at Duggy and Cammie.

Pidge snorted. Actually I was getting put clean through a window at the time!

What! said Billy. Everyone was laughing and cheering.

Fucking classic! shouted Duggy.

Did you not stand up to them? said Ray.

Aye, but only for about three seconds! Then they had me down, started to kick me and that, and then one of them, this big orange paisley top on, he says, Hold on lads, through the window with the cunt! And they drag me across the street, lift me up, swing me like a bag of tatties: A one! A two! A three! And the next thing I ken I'm in a fucking coma.

Fainted more like, muttered Cammie.

What?

Nothing.

Here's me lying on the floor with all this blood in my eyes, and broken glass and records all over the place: they'd chucked me through the window of the fucking Virgin Megastore!

Billy laughed.

Were you lifted? said Ray.

Och, one of them turned up at the hospital and speirt all the usual shite, but what could they do me for: head-butting a plate-glass window? I was the innocent victim.

Makes a change, eh! said Colin.

I'll tell you who gave me a real grilling though: my mother! I came into the house about half-ten: two black eyes – as you see – stitches all over the shop, my clothes all torn and covered in blood, and she looks me up and down and says, What time do you call this? Half-ten, I say. And where've you been till this time of night? Dundee Infirmary. WHAT? she screams, and she makes to clout me! Would've taken half my stitches out!

You didn't run from the Tayside Trendies, but you ducked your own ma, eh? Billy was laughing.

Beamer joined in. I can just see it, he said. Here son, what's that ambulance doing out in the road? Och, they gave me a hurl up from Dundee Mum, I said you'd pay the fare!

So you lost a lot of blood did you?

Too right I did, Ray. The doctors told me, Son, get out there and drink at least five pints immediately, or else your body's going to shrivel up like a dried-out johnny.

What does Adidas stand for? said Duggy.

Folk stopped laughing, there was a short silence.

What? said Cammie.

A durex is dead after sex!

No, but what was the question though?

Hih, I bet they told you to drink Guinness, eh Pidge?

Nah, red kola they said Ray, Guinness is the wrong colour.

But it's good for you though, I mean it's the most healthy drink you can get, it builds you up. That's how they give it to blood donors.

Everybody looked at Ray.

Away and shite, said Colin.

Nah, it's right enough, said Ray. Cause my mother goes to the blood transfusion, and she says she aye gets a half pint of Guinness afterwards: it fills up your veins again I suppose.

You can sell your blood in America, said Cammie. I saw a programme about it.

You can sell your spunk as well, said Beamer.

What?

Fuck off Beamboy!

You're joking man!

It's true, you sell it to a sperm bank. I read it.

Who'd want to buy your spunk anyway Beamer? said Colin.

I'm not saying mine just, but anybody's.

What, even some AIDS-ridden Jambo?

Well, I suppose they do tests Col . . .

Aye, I can just see it, said Colin. Now sir, are you an HIV

positive by any chance? You are? Well, that's fine. Hold on though . . . Hearts supporter? FUCK OFF!

What Beamer's saying is right enough, said Billy. I mean it's good to know: if you're really hard up you can always go and get paid a few quid for wanking into a test-tube. Or a two-litre beaker in my case!

Fuck off! everybody shouted.

I still don't see what they do with it once they've got it though, said Pidge.

Well, said Billy, You ken Tunnock's Tea Cakes . . . ?

Everybody laughed.

They say it's good for the skin, said Billy. I read that somewhere, gets rid of spots and that.

Ho ho, so that would explain why your Sandra hasn't had any plooks lately, said Colin.

Cammie sat up from where he was lying on the grass, knocking a few empty cans aside. I can just see you Billy, he said. Here Sandra, want to try some of my new face cream? He held his hand under his nose, sniffed at it, stared at the palm as if examining something there, then started to pat it over his cheeks and forehead.

Aye, said Colin, And the next stage is: Hey Sandra, I hear it's very good for mouth ulcers as well!

Everyone was laughing, except for Billy, and they were licking their lips at him, sticking their tongues out, and making jerk-off movements with their hands up at their mouths. Billy jumped to his feet.

Here, hold on a minute, he said. Just fucking . . . just, just fuck off you bastards! There was more laughter. Shut it cunts! This is my girlfriend you're fucking slagging here!

Who mentioned slags? shouted Duggy. Right enough, slag's the word!

He let out a shout of laughter, but already Billy had leapt

over in front of him, was bringing his leg back away to kick, leaning into it with the weight of his body. Colin was on his feet too, and as Billy began to swing, Colin was across and shoving him off his balance, Billy hytering away, Colin striding after him, pushing him down and onto his back on the short grass, standing over him, arms at his sides but fists clenched.

Stop right fucking there Billy boy! You watch who you're lifting your feet to, or I'll be lifting my hand to you: you'll be fucking stabbed you cunt . . .

Billy sat up, tried to get to his feet, but Colin raised his right foot, stuck his trainer right under Billy's nose. Billy could've grabbed it, twisted Colin to the ground, but he just looked at it, stopped rising, and then Colin placed his foot on Billy's shoulder, slowly leant forward on that leg, till Billy was forced to lie back again and flat out on the ground.

Billy's eyes were closed. His chest was heaving up and down. He opened his eyes, looked straight up into Colin's face.

Aye, fair enough, he said. But I can't have just anycunt going around miscalling my dame.

That's the point man Billy, that's the fucking point! You thick fucker! Aye, *anycunt* badmouthing Sandra fair enough, give them a belt across the fucking chops. Aye, *anycunt*. But not Duggy, nah, not any of the crew . . . your own fucking mob man! That's enemy-within stuff that is, that's the end of the Dyce Casual Crew if we start fighting amongst ourfuckingselves.

Billy lifted his head slightly and began to look slowly round the circle. Colin sniffed:

Tell him I'm right Cammie.

Well I would say you were right actually, to be honest.

Too right you're right, said Duggy. I mean if we're going to start battering each other we might . . .

Shut your gob, said Colin. Don't go fucking stirring it now, I'm trying to get your hash sorted out here.

He glowered around at Duggy and then the others as they sat or lay around drinking and smoking. He shook his shoulders, kind of shivering, then stepped away from Billy, moved over to where he'd left his can before the trouble. He paused, then bent to pick up the can, and swallowed the contents.

There's some more Kestrels over here, said Pidge.

Colin lowered the can from his lips, crumpled it in his hand, then chucked it onto the pile of empties that was growing in the centre of the circle. He was looking into the trees. Suddenly he turned back to Billy.

Come here with me man. Aye, Billy, come on.

Who, me?

Aye, you.

What, can I get up now?

Just shut it and get over here, okay? Colin moved away towards the edge of the clearing.

Billy sat up, leant back on his arms for a second, shaking his head, then stood up and followed Colin. The others watched them for a few moments, then started moving as well. Pidge and Cammie crawled over and grabbed a couple more cans each from where the carriers had been couped; Duggy davered out between two of the stones, down as far as the dyke surrounding the circle, then slowly walked further round the side of the knowe, gradually working his way up towards the top again; Beamer and Ray tagged after Colin to the far side of the circle. Here there was a massive brute of a stone, big as three of the others put together, and it was lying on its side inbetween two upright stones, touching them at each end. It was flat on the top, and Colin was leaning his elbow on it, staring at Billy and flicking his eyes over the rest of them as they approached. Billy stopped a couple of feet in front of him, hands in the pockets of his jeans;

23

Beamer and Ray were slightly behind Billy; Pidge and Cammie had got to their feet and were drinking and watching from a short distance away; the sound of Duggy fighting through branches and bracken was coming closer.

Listen, said Colin, and slapped his hand on the flat top of the big stone. See these bastards here, they're called the Devil Stanes, as I said before. A few of the others nodded. But. Who kens who put them here?

Eh, the devil? said Cammie.

Colin raised his eyes slowly to the sky, sighed, and said, Nah, they only got the name cause the farmers were ignorant feartie bastards a hundred-odd years ago. So not much has changed: I mean look at Duggy's father.

Duggy had been struggling up the back of the mound. Now he reached the top, and leant over the big stone, peching hard. What's that you're saying about my da? he said, looking up.

I was just talking about who put these stones here, said Colin.

Well it wasn't my da, said Duggy. His ground only comes as far round as the quarry, not up to here.

Colin looked at Duggy for a moment, then shook his head, curled his top lip in a kind of sarcastic smile. Well I'm glad we've got that sorted out, he said.

Was it the Picts? said Ray.

Not a bad guess Raymie, said Colin, But still completely fucking wrong. Nah, these things were here years before the Picts came along. These are Stone-Age stones, these are, fucking ancient history! These go back to the days of the druids – fucking two thousand BC man!

Everyone looked around at the circle. Colin waited a few seconds, then slapped his palm on the flat stone again, and nodded at it. Come on Billy, he said, Get up on here a minute.

What?

You heard me.

Eh?

Billy. Get up on this stone for a minute, I'm needing to show the lads something.

Billy kicked at a lump of grass a few times, then shrugged his shoulders. Fine by me, he said. He leant back against the side of the big stone, placed his hands on the edge of it behind him, elbows jabbing into the air. Fine by me, he said again. Then he straightened his arms and pulled himself up and back, scrabbling with his heels on the rough side of the stone at the same time. Then he was there, sitting on top of the big flat stone, his feet dangling a good eighteen inches off the ground. He looked around at the rest of the crew, smiling.

Now lie down, said Colin.

Billy snapped his head round, mouth open. What? he shouted. The others were laughing, apart from Colin. Colin was looking at Billy, unsmiling. Then he scratched his head, took a step back, and began to walk slowly round to the right, round the upright stone, and in behind the back of the flat one.

Shift! he said, and elbowed Duggy away from where he was leaning. Duggy wandered round to the other side, where Beamer and Ray were standing; Pidge and Cammie came closer too. All of them were looking at Col. Billy turned his head too.

Can I get down now? he said.

Don't move, said Colin quietly. Now listen. Back in the Stone Age, right, when the druids were on the go, and they put up this stone circle here, how many of them do you think it took? He glanced around, but nobody made to answer. Well I'll tell you for nothing: it wasn't a couple of mates that got drunk one night and decided to cart the buggers up here just for a laugh. No fucking way. It was a big job. Look at the size of this thing! He spread his arms out along the length of the flat stone; his fingertips were still a couple of feet away from the upright stones at each end. See that? Must weigh twenty ton at least – more! And they'd no fucking JCBs in them days.

And all these others as well, said Pidge, looking round at the smaller stones that made up the circle.

Must've taken a hell of a lot of druids to hump these things all the way up here, said Beamer.

Exactly! cried Colin, and smacked both his hands down. Team work, that's what it was! The Druid Mental Crew in action: fifty lads pushing from behind, another fifty pulling with ropes, all the way up the fucking brae! Sweaty work, Christ aye, but they stuck in, they had the fucking dedication, dedication to howk them out of the ground God knows where, drag them away up here, then plant them in the ground again!

Sounds pretty daft to me, said Duggy. They'd've saved themselves a lot of bother if they'd just set them up in a circle wherever they found them.

Aye, or at least they could've stuck them down by the river or something, said Ray. I mean it was bad enough coming up here with two bags of carry-out.

Ah well, that's the whole point, said Colin. Hih, Billy, lie down a minute, will you?

I tellt you: no.

Oh, okay. Anyway, they had to put the circle up here, cause there was a lot of mental violence going on, and you had to be able to see the country all around, to make sure nobody was sneaking up on your ceremonies and that.

Ceremonies? said Pidge. What, you mean like devil worship and that? Black Sabbath fans were they?

The devil wasn't even invented then, said Beamer. Is that not right man? It was the sun and the moon and that they worshipped, eh? We did it in history, mind Col?

Colin glowered at him, then cleared his throat and went on, Aye, that's another reason for having the circle up here. They had to have a good view of the stars and the sunset and stuff, so they'd ken when to do their various ceremonies, and their HUMAN SACRIFICE!

As he shouted, Colin jumped forward and grabbed Billy's shoulders, and pulled him down backwards. Billy's head thunked onto the stone. Jesus fuck! he shouted, and began to struggle to sit up, and to clutch at the back of his head. But Colin was holding both his arms, pinning his shoulders down.

Grab his fucking feet, said Colin.

Nobody moved, except Billy, who began to thrash his legs about.

CAMMIE! PIDGE! GET A HOLD OF HIS FUCKING FEET! shouted Colin.

The two of them moved forward.

Stop waving your legs about a minute, said Pidge.

Billy made a spluttering noise half-way between a laugh and a snort and some watery bogies shot out his nose onto his top lip, then ran down his cheeks, one dripple each side. He stopped kicking.

Hold him down, said Colin. Now, he said, Move him round so he's lying longways.

Billy's body went very stiff, all his muscles tightening, his legs and arms stretching straight out, but he wasn't struggling any more. They half-lifted and half-dragged him till he was lying out along the length of the flat stone, his head touching one upright stone and his feet just short of the other. His eyes were staring straight upwards. Colin leant over Billy's face and grinned down at him. Then he pursed his lips, pushed them together and out in a kissing movement.

You wouldn't, said Billy.

Wouldn't what? said Colin, smiling.

You haven't even got your blade with you. Why should you?

Don't you worry about me and my friend Mr Stanley, said Colin. We can look after ourselves okay. He laughed quietly, and looked up at the others. They nodded and grinned as they saw him glancing round, then went back to frowning, looking worried. Duggy, Beamer, Ray, said Colin. Come in close. They shuffled forward.

What's the score Col? said Pidge. How long've we got to hold him down for?

Not long, said Col. Just till I've finished. The corners of his mouth were upturned, the teeth showing, but the skin around his eyes was smooth. I've got something to say to you, you see, all of you, and Billy especially. Listen. Colin shifted his hands off Billy's shoulders, lifting one free into the air, and moving the other over to hold Billy's throat. This squabble theday, he said, The wee ruckus between Duggy and Billy here, well, we can't have that kind of thing going on in the Dyce Casual Crew. He shook his head. The only folk who get anything done in this world are the folk that stick together, that work together. Like the fucking druids dragging these rocks up the fucking hill. Now if they'd been fighting amongst themselves, they'd never've done nothing. Agreed? Now. What was this fight about theday?

Duggy started slagging my dame . . .

SHUT UP! shouted Colin, and brought his free hand down to press along with the other on Billy's throat. LISTEN! This fight, and a couple of others recently, they've all been caused by one thing and one thing only. And what's that? Women: the fucking hairies've been at the back of it all.

There was a stirring of noise amongst the lads.

Aye, like you just on Friday, Pidge. We were supposed to be discussing tactics for yesterday, and what happens? You piss off to the pictures with – what's her name?

Eh, Colleen. Aye.

Colleen, you go to the pictures with Colleen. Okay, that's fine, no law against that, I mean she's a tasty bit of stuff, nobody's denying it. But: you went out with her on Thursday night as well! Now then, that's just totally out of order. Two nights in a row!

Christ, that's as good as married, said Billy.

Colin ignored him. It's simple, he said. Either you go out with her or with the boys, simple as that. You can't do both.

Pidge shrugged. I ken, usually, he said. But I was just getting her warmed up on the Thursday, ken? I mean she was pretty randy-radge already: just about sucking my tongue out of its socket, just about swallowing my fucking head! And on Friday she says, Do you want to come back to my place then? My folks are out ... And I say, So nobody's in, eh? And she says, Aye, nobody except my wee brother and my big sister looking after him. But I mean, if it hadn't been for them I reckon ...

Pidge, said Colin, You've proved my point. Once you get stuck on some lassie you're finished: you become a totally boring bastard, dancing up and down like her fucking yo-yo. Save it! We're not interested in your sex life! He paused, staring at Pidge, breathing heavily.

Sex, said Billy.

Shut up you, said Colin.

No, it's interesting, said Billy in a husky voice, his throat still constricted. Never mind Pidge though. Come on Col and tell us about your sex life.

Don't fucking start, said Colin. Don't, just don't ...

Ach, don't be shy man, come on: the full juicy details: names and places Col, points out of ten, let's have it!

No! Fuck ... what ... Colin's eyelids were trembling, and one corner of his mouth was twitching up into his cheek.

If you're too modest, Col, I'll just have to tell the lads all about it myself . . .

Colin's head jerked back. His lips were moving, but no sound was coming out. He glanced down at Billy, then quickly jerked his head away again, and froze. He slowly closed his eyes, held them clenched shut for ten seconds, then opened them again, opened them very wide.

Billy raised his arms from his sides and moved his hands up around Colin's wrists, as if to prise the fingers away from his throat. But before Billy touched them, Colin loosened his grasp and lifted his hands up and away. He lifted them up to his head, rested them on top of it for a moment, then dragged them down over his face and rubbed his eyes with his fingertips.

Billy sat up. Immediately, Cammie and Pidge let go of his ankles and stepped off backwards. Billy swung round till his legs were hanging over the side of the stone, the same side Colin was standing at, then he slid forward on the arse of his jeans and dropped onto the ground beside Colin.

Colin had let his hands fall from his face, but he wasn't looking at anyone. He stared at the top of the stone where Billy had been lying.

Billy turned and leant over the stone, and spoke. I think what wee Col here is trying to say is this: he's no chance of getting a ride for at least three years – I mean look at him, he's a scrotty wee runt – and *we've* all got to live like monks till *his* balls drop and he gives us the nod, Okay to get your hole now lads! Well fuck that for a game of soldiers! Billy laughed. I'm fucked if I'm going to live like a fucking druid, no sex and carrying boulders all over the fucking shop! I tell you Col, if the druids are so fucking magic and clever, where are they theday, eh? Tell me that? Why are they not here now telling us to get the fuck out of their stone circle, off of their patch? Here's why: cause they're fucking extinct, they died out man! And why? Cause they were too knackered from dragging standing stones about to shag their birds when they got home. They never fucking grew up! And that's not going to happen to me. I'm off.

Billy looked at Colin for a few seconds, then stepped away from him, round the side of the stone and into the middle of the circle. He stopped. I'm going down the High Street, he said. Anybody coming? Nobody moved. Billy shook his head. Well fuck the lot of you, he said. You'll be down sooner or fucking later. He turned and strode off, out the far side of the circle, down the slope and over the dyke. The others watched as he walked away across the park.

Ray cleared his throat. Actually, I think I'll go with him, he said.

Eh, if you're going . . . I'll chum you down, said Beamer.

Colin focused on the crew for the first time, glowered round at them all. No one spoke. Ray and Beamer picked up their jackets and followed after Billy. As they started to climb over the dyke, Duggy shuffled his feet and took a couple of steps in the direction they'd headed, but almost immediately he stopped, turned, took a couple of steps back. He glanced over in Colin's direction, then looked away at a tree growing out of the side of the knowe; it had been half blown-over at some point, and its trunk was jammed at an angle against the next tree down the slope. Its roots were half rugged out of the earth, looking dried-up and grey hanging there in the air.

Are you going then? said Colin.

Duggy started. Who, me? he said. Colin was staring at him. He shrugged, nodded, then shook his head. Nah, Billy's a wanker, he said. I'll stay here. I mean there must be a few cans still to be drunk . . .

Have a look, said Colin.

Duggy went over to where the carriers had been couped out, picked up a couple of cans there, then got a few more from the far side of the circle, where someone had made a second stockpile when they first arrived. He came back over, and set the cans up in a row on top of the flat stone. There were five of them.

Well, said Colin, Is anybody else pissing off?

Not me, said Duggy. Cammie and Pidge shook their heads.

Well that's one each then, said Colin.

And one extra, said Pidge.

I was just fucking coming to that, said Colin.

Well, who gets it? said Cammie. Do we share it out, get a gulp each like? I mean that would be fair after what you were saying about teamwork and that.

Ken this, said Colin, I'm glad those three cunts've buggered off. I've been worried about them for a while. They were getting weak, losing their bottle. And if we're going to be the toughest in battle, the hardest mob in Aberdeen – and that means in the country – we can't have any slackers. If we're going to keep our self-respect, keep our name as the mentallest team around, it has to be all or nothing.

So who gets the extra can? said Duggy.

I do, said Colin. Any complaints?

GORDON LEGGE

Neighbours

Sammy had had enough. He flung the pillow at the wall and got himself out of bed.

For years now this had been going on. Oh, he'd been round before. Up in the middle of the night and giving them a piece of his mind. He'd written to the council and he'd telephoned the police, but still it made no difference. They just did as they pleased, that lot.

Tonight, though, tonight Sammy would give them a scare . . . The rolling-pin! He'd take the rolling-pin.

Sammy checked himself in the mirror. The rolling-pin was easily concealed in his dressing-gown pocket and could be withdrawn in a flash. Brilliant.

There was no rain and the night was still as Sammy headed out. The only observer was a prowling cat who dived for cover upon seeing Sammy.

Chap! Chap!

Sammy couldn't resist it. He withdrew the rolling-pin from his pocket and held it above his head, ready to frighten the living daylights out of whoever answered the door.

This was as much as the gateman of the oil refinery needed to see before slamming the door shut again and dialling 999.

Clumsy

It was the bruises. Big black and blue things on her wrists. I've not seen her. Nobody's seen her. Don't know what she's playing at. Nothing happened. I mean, Paul was through the room, for Christ's sake. Okay, he was pished out his brain, but it's not as if we were alone. I was just wanting to party. There was nothing in it. I mean, it's not as if I don't like her. I mean, I really like her.

Shame

It was out of order, bringing up a debt, bringing up a debt in front of mates. You don't do things like that. I haven't forgotten. He'll get his money. That's what I hate. Folk like that. Makes out like he's desperate for it. Comes in raving away about this brand new mountain bike, the next thing he's asking me about that fiver. I had to leave. Couldn't handle it. First time in weeks I've been out and I had to leave. I had to leave the best part of half a pint. Says it doesn't matter. Whenever I've got myself sorted out'll do. Nice one that. Yeah, Mr Nice Guy, nice one, and some folks just need their legs broke eh.

Our Donna

No, but our Donna's got it made. Christ, even her teachers are saying it. Oh aye, her mam's right into it. It's Donna-this, Donna-that, and Hell mend the rest of you. Quite right too. No, the lassie's got that wee bit of class about her. So what if all her eggs've to be double-yolked? That's the way I see it. You've got to spoil them when they're like that. It'll be worth it, though. Too right it'll be worth it. Just you keep an eye out cause I'm telling you here and now, any money, Page Three within a year.

Life on a Scottish Council Estate Vol 2 Chap 1

There's a knock at my door. It's one of my neighbours. He says 'Gordon, fancy coming through and sorting out our Campbell's homework for him?' 'What is it this time?' I says. 'Och, some mince for Burns Night. Come on through. I'll stand you a coffee and a fag.' 'Lead the way,' I says and follows him through. In the kitchen his wife is attending to the baby. My neighbour says, 'See getting that bairn off to his bed, Gordon. You've no idea what it's like. That right, hen?' His wife agrees. She says 'He's a wee besom, Gordon, so he is.' I laughs and says 'What is this homework, anyway?' My neighbour picks up the homework book and says, 'Oh aye, what it is is, he's to write down ten Scottish words . . . Gordon, what's a Scottish word?'

First Day at Work

'Why'd you not catch it?' said the guy who looked like Plug out the Beano as the axe struck George just above the elbow, slicing off the best part of his arm.

The Joy of Knowledge

Ah ken ivry cunt. Ivry las bastarn bastard fi this sorry fucking shitehole. Ken wha's a zoomer, ken wha's a cling-oan n ken wha's a Rod. Ken aw wha ah wiz it skill wi, ken aw wha ah've wirkd wi nken aw wha ah've met – cuz ah mind ivry cunt. Ken ma famely, ken ma freens n ken ma neebours – ken ther's tae. Ken wha's fi wher nwha's no here i.e. wha's in the hoaspital n wha's in the jile. Fuck it, ah ken ivry cunt.

Life

She always made a joke of what it was like to be small. Then one day I made a mistake when I told her to stop selling herself short. I realised this was a mistake before the bread-knife entered between my ribs but it didn't seem to matter.

JAMES MEEK

The Oxford Book of Shopping and Fucking

There's so much to see and do in this strange, mad, wonderful world.

A golden life is waiting for you, just over the horizon. If you could only grab it with both hands, make it yours, and never let it go.

A rich lifestyle of choice and security – who can stop you when you're young and talented, with a hunger to make it to the top?

Unfortunately there is somebody.

Somebody low, and small, with nothing better to do than get in your way.

It may be a tenant who won't be evicted. It may be a troublemaker complaining about low pay. It may simply be an old sex partner talking to the newspapers.

That's why we're here. At British Violence we can help free your life from these little people.

We can take them out and tidy them up. Bully, beat and murder these awkward customers so that you can carry out your business in perfect peace of mind.

BRITISH VIOLENCE

We hurt them so they can't hurt you.

Someone Would Have to Go

After the drivers agreed to give up the union they didn't get a pay rise for a couple of years. They talked about it a lot and complained to the garage manager but he shrugged and said it was nothing to do with him. Eventually it was stated by a number of drivers in the pub that someone would have to go up to the main office and ask one of the directors about it. Nobody wanted to be the one to go so they all wrote their names on bits of beermat, put them in a hat and shook them up. Shona picked a name out. It was Jim, Jim Hartwell.

Next day he came in hoping everyone would have forgotten about it but they hadn't. He was expected to go. He asked the garage manager if he could use the phone to call the main office but he couldn't. So he got dropped off up there in his lunch break and asked his way to the directors' office. He asked if he could speak to someone about the fact they hadn't had a pay rise for a couple of years. A secretary said he wanted the deputy managing director. She made an appointment for his lunch break the following week.

Jim came back the following week and got shown through to the deputy managing director's office.

– Sit down, said the deputy managing director, pointing to a low leather armchair. Jim sank into it. Now, said the deputy managing director, what can I do for you?

– It's just about the pay, you know, said Jim. We haven't had an increase for a couple of years.

– I see, said the deputy managing director. Would you excuse me a moment. He lifted one of his telephones and dialled a short number. Hello, he said, could you send someone up, please. He put the phone down. Won't be a moment, he said.

A security guard entered the room. The deputy managing director said to Jim: I'm sorry, what was your name?

– Jim Hartwell.

The deputy managing director turned to the security guard. Could you escort Mr Hartwell from the building, please, and be sure he never enters the company's premises again, he said.

DUNCAN McLEAN

Thistle Story

On my way to the pub one evening I passed a public call box. It was full of thistles.

I stopped and looked more closely. It was a perfectly normal phonebox on the outside but the inside was stacked full of thistles, right to the roof. Some of the thistles near the ground looked crushed, but the ones at eye level were crisp and green, prickles glistening in the light of a nearby street lamp. Some of them had wee tartan ribbons twisted round their stalks in bows.

I looked up and down the street: there was no one about. Who had put them in there? I had no idea.

Just then, the phone started to ring. I couldn't get in to answer it because the box was full of thistles.

Fair Play

That's not fair! I would cry, as my Dad cheated at Monopoly again.

Life's not fair, he would reply, slipping another hotel onto Park Lane.

The Big Man That Dropped Dead

I had this pal that knew about poetry, he was in the mental asylum. He could speak poetry really good, in fact he couldn't speak anything else. He'd see it up there and he'd just pull it down and speak it. On and on. He dropped dead though. I was standing there and he fell down right in front of me. Aye he was a big man, but he just dropped dead. So there you go, eh, poetry . . .

ALISON KERMACK

A Poyum

It wiz a weerd wee boax.
Sorty lozinj shaped
wi a padloak oan it
whaze keez wur inna safe
whaze combinayshun wiz inna cumpyootur
whaze code wiz in the heedy
the heedy the lichrachur dipartmin.

It took a wee while
anna loatty purswayshin
bit ivenshully
thay geed mi a wee keek
inside.

Wastey time
kiz aw thit wiz thayr
wiz a piley dustin ashiz
whit yoosty be
a poyum.

iffyd gonty MA skule . . .

thayrz that fukn weerdo
fukn toap marx agayn
arslickur
lets batturum

oy
shaykspeer ya kunt
shoatty

Non Sequitur

thatsa loady pish

how kin yi say
am fuckn thick
jiss kiz ah dinny ken
whit a non-fuckn-sekwitur is

thurs prolly hunners i peepul
dinny ken that
disny meanty say
thur aw thick

yir tokin bawlicks

Thrown Out

in between
the two rows
of houses

no

in between
the wall of the house
and the rubbish bags

no

in between
the rubbish bags

no

in between the rubbish

no

in between
the rub
and the bish

lies
the auld yin

The Perfect Soldier

Awright.
Soave gotta skinheed
anna wear dox.
Awright.
Soah treat burds like shite
screw
whatever akin git.
Awright.
Soave bin inna bitty bother
whatwi poofbashn
an pakkybashn
an the B.N.P. marches.
Awright.
So ma eyes are set
that far back inma heed
ah canny see
where the fuck am gawn.

But ah meenty say.

Ken whot that Careers Kunt
sayed tay mi?
Ken whot that Daft Basturt
actually sayed?

Says ad be
The Perfick Soajer.
Says ah should join
the fuckn Army.

Meenty say
day ah look like

the sorty fanny
wid put onna uniform
anday whit am telt.

Fuckn deformayshunny
character
thasswhit that is.

Bemused

1. Losing It

Ah says
ahm rytin lyk a basturt.
She says
exkyooz mee?
I said
I'm writing like a bastard.
She said
beg pardon?
I said
My Muse Is Upon Me.

She said
thats better.
More poetic.
More befitting
a woman.

2. Finding It

I said
My Muse Is Upon Me.
She said
what?
Ah says
ma myooz iz upoan mi.
She says
whit?
Ah says
ahm rytin lyk a basturt.

She says
aw, rite, thats gid.
Wundurd whit
yi wur tockin aboot.

Ah says I.
Ah wundurd masel.

Culture Versus Convention

punctuation: ya Basturt ahll give ye fukn punk.choo;ay-
shun, Daft Kunt. I ah ken itsa SEE ah ken that . . . dinny
tokty ME aboot fukn spelln. arsehole. whidjimeen noa
proper sentins, whot, fukn GRAMMAR noo izzit fer
fuxake. Aw sorry pal, izma langwich butherin ye? I well
naebdy tolt ye then its awrite. its awrite see cozzam rytin
a fukn poyum.

Dislekseeah

isslike wee wurrums
the boy said
isslike, ken the wuns,
they wurrums
thats oan thi payvmin
efter its bin raynin
an they croll
offy thi grass
onty thi payvmin
an yi olwaze hufty
wok cayrfull
case ye stanoan thum
nskwosh thum
thass whit thi wurdzizlike
oan thi payj
thasswhit thurlike
tay me

thur olwaze riggilin aboot

ocht,
they wurrums,
thur jist trine
tay git back tay thi grass.

JANICE GALLOWAY

Part of Foreign Parts

> Normandy is an agricultural region, full of farms and mead-
> owland, orchards and endless pasture to produce the excel-
> lent dairy produce for which the region is justly famous.
> Normandy is a place to explore and take time over, full of
> echoes of the Viking past and peasant or fishing present.
> Merchants, pilgrims and sightseers have thronged here since
> the 11th Century.

There was no mention of the war.

Cassie read it again and flipped over a couple of pages
about Historic Rouen and beautiful cathedrals, women wearing headdresses and the charm of old marketplaces. The
adjoining map was raddled with crosses but there was no
mention of the bloody war.

Out the window, there were just yards of FLAT.

It was flatter than Holland for godsakes. FLAT FOR
MILES.

And there was no mention of how it got that way, shelled
and reshelled over the same yards of ground in some cases.
No acknowledgement. Cassie looked up from the page and
there was Rona, driving away. Oblivious, the flat muddiness
stretching out through the glass behind her driving arm. Rona
just didn't notice.

It's flat because of the war.

Rona did nothing.
The war. They bombed it all to hell and that's why
    it's so flat.
Rona squinted quick out her side window.
Look. Cows.

Cassie stopped breathing for a moment. Rona meant it. She
didn't often offer conversation when she was driving but she
was probably more used to the other side of the road by now.
It wouldn't be worth getting incredulous about the cow remark,
pushing the war thing instead. Cassie watched Rona's hands on
the wheel and felt suddenly tender. Cassie couldn't even imagine
the other side of the road thing, how it was managed. Right and
left were alien concepts. They were unable to be explained and
not open to reason. They just were what they were. You either
knew them or you didn't and Cassie didn't. Rona knew left and
right, port and starboard and the points of the compass. It was
probable she could tell when they were near running water and
whether enemy horses were coming by putting her ear to the
ground and listening. Rona was that sort. A survivor. Cassie
looked at Rona's hands on the wheel then back at her own.
Helpless as dead fish. Unable to drive. She was the passenger,
being hurtled over strange terrain down an unkent side of the
road, not able to check whether it was the right one. If Rona
was making mistakes she just wouldn't know. It was dizzying,
really. Instead, Cassie watched Rona animal spotting, her hands
doing their thing. It was eerie the way Rona could drive for
miles and not really be focused on anything, not even be awake.
Sometimes driving to the office in the mornings she would say
O we're here when she was turning into the carpark like it was
a surprise. And there was that same expression; coming round
from a dead faint. Rona shook her head from side to side and
said it again.

See? Cows, and pointing. Cassie looked and saw only mist. Her eyes needed wiping. She rubbed them in a way she hoped suggested lack of sleep and tried again. Rona snorted.

You didn't look in time. You missed them.

Smug. Cassie said nothing.

You could look for the signs to Chantilly. Or maybe I should look at the map. Want a coffee?

It wasn't just the cows, then. She was getting lively thinking about coffee.

Ok.

You look for somewhere then. Tell me.

Cassie watched a big wooden crate with petrol pumps outside float past the window.

Was that something?

No. Cassie hated questions like that. They didn't have a sensible answer.

We could stop there.

We could. On the other hand maybe we won't.

It might be ok. The car was slowing down.

There'll be other places.

I could stop though. Whatever you think. The car was still slowing down.

No. I don't want to be involved in any turning back. Just keep going. I said there would be other –

But I could turn back easy, it's no bother.

I didn't say it would be bother. I said I didn't want any turning back.

Jesusjesus.

Cassie knew she was in the wrong but it was infuriating anyway. Rona never listened. Only here – what the hell time was it? Cassie read the watch on Rona's wrist surreptitiously rather than be seen looking at her own. It said seven forty-five.

Only here an hour and fifteen minutes and something like a
fight was having to be avoided. First days were always the
same: competition for Injured Silence and who was ahead
on the Cow Count. But they were driving on. Rona lifted
her wrist, examined what time it was, probably she had seen
Cassie looking and didn't want to miss anything. You couldn't
even be surreptitious without Rona noticing. Rona resettled the
watch hand on the wheel then lifted it again, fumbling round the
side of her seat and into the horse bag, rooting for something. It
made it near impossible to drive straight or even see out but she
kept at it till she found whatever the hell it was. Something white
held in the hand when she straightened up again, jerking at the
last minute to avoid the kerb. A polomint. Jesus a polomint.
She could have totalled the car looking for the bloody thing.
Leaving Cassie sitting there, knowing what it meant. It meant
Rona didn't need her even to fetch a bloody sweetie from the
bottom of her bag. Anything rather than ask. She never bloody
asked. Cassie looked out the window again. Tension was making
her thighs hurt. At the side of the road, a lone woman was trying
to thumb a lift. You could watch her approach, come level,
retreat. From behind, her whole back and a foot above her head
was consumed by backpack. She didn't as much as turn to see
if they had slowed. Cassie watched the reflection of the woman
in the vanity mirror over the passenger-seat eyeshade. It was so
flat you could see her grow smaller for miles. Or imagined you
could. Miles.

She felt the car skidding even before she woke. Her neck
was too hot, being sawn across by a heavy ray of sun. Dust
filled up the side windows, rising from where the tyres would
be.

Here we are.

Rona was doing something, ferreting for her purse, the

roadmap, one of the two shoulderbags. She switched the igni-
tion off. They were getting out. Rona's door opening, her
seat sighing with shifting weight. Cassie blinked against the
too-brightness and swallowed to ease the dry throat. Sleeping
with her mouth open again. The soreness at the top of her
back when she tried to lift her head and the eyelids seamed
with leadshot. Rona already banging the door and chapping on
the window then looking up at the sky open-eyed. Her mouth
freshly scented with mint. Cheery as hell.

Dark.
Like the place had no idea it was morning outside. Bulbs were
on somewhere in the recessed interior. Four men in teeshirts
with paunches over the belt bands and spaghetti stains on the
fronts of their teeshirts hung about in front of the counter. The
dull hissing noise might have been coming from the stoury
radio over the gantry. Anything else, like giant flies, didn't bear
thinking about. No one was saying anything. It wasn't just from
outside, then. The cafe looked like hell from inside as well: tables
cluttered up too close together and the four men with stomachs.
Cassie tried not to look at anyone. Or the stains. Or anything.
The stomachs quivered when the men breathed in. This was
short change. Frenchmen were supposed to be sauve.
Two of them looked over then looked away. Cassie's face felt
peeled. By the time she raised her eyes again, a different man
was scrutinising Rona's back as she sloped past on a scouting
mission for a toilet. Then back. She felt for the novel in her back
pocket, tried to look collected. The novel was a standard tactic:
something to affect distance with, pretending to be fascinated
by the cover photo or the insides depending on how desperate
things were. Therese Raquin jesus Zola. Zola in translation.
There was a horrible moment of cold sweat while she wondered
if it would attract conversation. But no one would notice or if

they did, care. No one came to take an order either, so it was probably the kind of place where you did it yourself and that was fine because it left more time to think up how to cope with making the order at all. But terrible because it left her sitting doing nothing after walking into a cafe. They would think she was an idiot. Worse. An English female idiot. They always thought you were English. It was usually possible to last out though. She lasted out till Rona came back smiling, bumping into a table.

I didn't order.

It seemed best to say before Rona reached the chair. Rona sighed and retraced a step or so then went to the counter. Right between the men who were waiting. The man behind the counter needed a shave.

Frenchmen were supposed to be suave.

They were supposed to have close-shaved clean chins and have those mesomorphic outlines, suggestion of muscles rippling through the polo shirt sleeves, neat little crocodile effect belts and pleated trousers, clever haircuts with side-partings and a flop of dark hair over the one eye. Lopsided grins. Yves St Laurent or Chanel uncurling from manly necks, discreet watches braceleting biteable wrists. But there were only these four men with stains and a man needing a shave. Too much hair. Cassie couldn't look. The nape of her neck was crawling.

> Frenchmen were supposed to be suave.
> Turkish men were sexcrazed.
> Scots were dour but could fuck all night.

Her spine was making ripples all the way down to her crotch. Rona's thin voice, half an octave higher than usual and asking for coffees in wounded French. Cassie couldn't look. There were cracks on the facing wall and dirt along the picture rail, the cocooned grey corpse of something a spider would come back for later wavering on a thin wire. Cassie thought about stalls. You got them in France: roadside stalls with fruit. It wouldn't be so bad there. Seven whateveritwas in the bloody morning. They could ask for some apples and maybe a melon, they could have bought their bloody breakfast there and that would have saved having to do this in the first place. But Rona arrives triumphant with two tiny cups. Flushed. Cassie knew they would drink the coffee, warding off the impending tip question and whether they would leave one, how much. Foreign countries jesus. Eight o five. An interminable two weeks of this to come.

They drank the coffees quick and in silence. Rona paid. One of the four men belched when she walked past, beginning to untangle the 500F note from the purse, getting ready the smile for foreigners. She didn't even notice. Cassie noticed though. She didn't want to but she noticed. All the men had hair on their arms. Thick enough to hide the skin colour. Beetling down over the backs of their hands. Cassie knew she had noticed enough. Cassie needed to go outside.

Outside smacked her eyes to slits. She had forgotten how bright it had been. She walked to the car, knowing it was shut. It was getting worse, this thing. This inability to speak or be at ease somewhere strange. Surely to god she wasn't always like this, this whatever it was. Surely it would only be a matter of time before

before

before what. Before something else. Before she was different.

55

Or the same as some previous time she couldn't quite remember. All she was sure of was that it had to be able to get better. The car looked dusty already, unpleasant. And locked. Rona had both sets. Rona always did. But soon she would come and open up the doors. They would get into the car and get moving again, maybe listen to some music. That's what they would do. They would listen to it and feel

They would feel

Cassie didn't know what they would feel but it might be better. Hair on their arms. One with a gold ring almost submerged on one finger. Thick black hair. Her neck was still riffling when she heard Rona's sandals coming. She didn't turn round. Through the window, she could see the personal stereo was there, under the travel kettle and two bags of bags. Rona thought polythene bags would be useful for things that needed to be kept separate like washing. The personal stereo but no tapes. But it would be a matter of minutes, seconds even before Rona started the car, like physical joy, the car starting to move, the simple thrill of a tyre dunting off the gravel and onto the road thank god for tarmac and the Romans the road the road moving again and no stops to worry about for a while. Only the one coffee so no need to worry about stopping for toilets either. She would put on the headphones even with no tape and listen to the hiss of the empty reels turning, stare out at the sky. Everything was fine so long as they were moving. Keeping going along the road

the road
the road
the road.

Flat fields and the bombsite remains. Cows and rabbits and flat fields, Normandy butter brewing inside those fourfold bovine guts from the green bit over the top of the flatness. Apple trees. Flat wasteland that had greened over again, things trying to recover from the bombed-to-hellness it had once been. In the distance, Cassie made out things like huge fingertips poking over the tops of the whitewashed wall. A sign.

Canadian Cemetery.

Rona looked keen but said nothing.

You never think of Canadians in the First World War. All that way. You never think of Canadians at all I suppose.

Cassie looked back at the stone tips. You didn't know how to react to it, whether it had nothing to do with you. Whether you were supposed to want to stop and see or whether that was just crass. Most of the stones wouldn't have names. Just collective obelisks to bits of strewn Canadian. Then the flatness came back, the cows and the trees dredging up sap from the ground to make cider and that brandy stuff. Calvados. Australian Cemetery. The map was covered in crosses. You spotted one cemetery and suddenly the rest were visible on the page, crosses floating to the surface like barley rising to the top of boiling soup. Canadians and Australians for godsake, stuck out here in this flatness and being processed into Calvados by the apple trees. Cassie stared at the turned earth of the nearside field. Australians to christ. Sucked dry by tree roots. All those dessicated Australian husks at the side of the road. She wanted to shut her eyes. Rona smiled and her lips moved. Cassie reached for the headphones.

GORDON LEGGE

Body Language

Always fidgeting they are. Christ, mean to say you've never noticed? It's either they've something in their eyes, or they're playing with their hair, or it's the clothes. Oh aye, always adjusting their clothes. All the time, man. Always at it. Telling you. Look, take that one. That one there. Give it a minute and you'll see what I mean. Just wait. Hold on. Just be like me, just watch her.

In Confidence

Hey, don't look, but mind I was on about that boy that's supposed to be moving into your close? . . . Him that's supposed to be some kind of mass-murderer? . . . Well, there you go, just this second come through the door's the brother of the lassie that was telling our Joyce about him.

Granny Goes Spare

Once a week I get my tea round at my Granny McIntyre's.

As gratitude for this I stay and keep her company while she watches her programmes. My Granny McIntyre says she can take or leave her programmes these days. They're all rubbish, anyway, she says. It's funny she says that – cause you should see the state of her when I put on the teletext to keep up with the midweek scores.

Bummed Out

Shona says
To say she's sorry
She hopes
You understand
Says to say
She'll stop and speak
But only
As a friend

A Bit Much

I've packed in with my psychiatrist. He was saying I should stop going round thinking everybody hates my guts . . . It was the way he said it, like.

Life on a Scottish Council Estate Vol 2 Chap 3

So I'm through next door babysitting again last night and the kids're asking if I'll lend them a hand with their homework. Aye, sure, no problem. What it is is they've been asked to work out the exact number of seconds that there are in any given year, right. Piece of piss, eh? So I gets one of their roughbooks and shows them all the relevant calculations and comes up with the answer, you know. Aye, but they're saying I'm wrong. I've got it wrong. Oh aye, my answer's nowhere near the one they're expecting. Nowhere near. They tells us I should try and work out the number of seconds for a leap year – cause according to the kids, right, this is supposed to give us the exact same answer . . . Me, I'm like this, just shaking the old head and thinking to myself, Dunderheid city, man. But, fair enough, if that's what they want, that's what they'll jolly well get. So I goes back, right back, and does all my calculations for the number of seconds in a day again – dead slow, like, you know, taking the pan and that – then I goes and adds this onto the total for the normal year, to make up the leap year, right. No, but, Christ, you should see them, see the faces on them, oh the kids are far from happy. Not happy at all. The answer's to be the same. The answer's got to be the same. No question. Now by this time I'm getting a wee bit fed up. A wee bit narked. So, drastic measures, I goes and gets their big blackboard and I hauls the bastarn brute through. Right, I says, right. From the top. Take it from the top. And I goes through it all as before: all the sums; all the multiplying; all the adding; everything; everything for both cases – and – surprise, surprise, lo and behold – I gets the exact same bloody answers as I got before. No, but the kids're still saying I'm wrong. I've got to be wrong cause they've been told the answer's to be the same in both cases – and the answer's to be twelve. Twelve! Twelve?

I goes like that. Just like this. Stunned. So I gets the old watch off the old wrist, right, and tells them, just tells them, to follow the second hand . . . Doosh! Doosh! Doosh! . . . Right, right all the way up to twelve . . . Doosh! Doosh! Doosh! That's it! That's how long twelve seconds takes. So there's going to be a damn sight more than twelve seconds in a year, that right? No, says the kids. There's only twelve, they say. There's only twelve seconds in a year. I'm just chucking it in. Shaking the head and that, you know. That's it. Finished. And it's then they start this giggling carry-on. I goes, what's the script with you pair then? There's only twelve, they say. There's only twelve seconds in a year. I've given it up. I'm away. No, they say, listen. Think about it. Just think about it. Cause there's the second of January, the second of February, second of March . . .

Gyp

There's a way folk have of judging
From an instance they remember
And your character's condemned
Through this lapse in behaviour
In the way you get acknowledged
And you're introduced to others
As the man who leaves his wallet
Where he leaves his working trousers

The Change

Look at it. You've got all these young lassies living on their lonesome bringing up the wee ones. Not a man to be seen. Right bloody tremendous it is. Never like that in my day. Nah, I had to marry that fucking bitch.

Not Proven

You ask our Rab, he'll tell you all I says was, 'You never noticed how men always try to impress you with agreeing with everything you say, but how women always try to impress you by disagreeing with everything you say?' and she went right fucking mental, she did.

BRENT HODGSON

A Lesson

Teacher:	Hallo bhoys and ghirls.
Children:	Hallo Captain Miss Mercer.
Teacher:	Today we are learning the Quantum Theory.
Children:	Mister Schrodinger put a cat into a box which was sealed. Inside the box was a pellet of poison and a sardine; then he connected up a supply of oxygen and went to bed with the cleaning lady.
Teacher:	He was a brave man, wasn't he children?
Children:	Yes Sir, Captain Miss Mercer.
Teacher:	What happened next children? To the cat?
Children:	O sir!
Teacher:	This is a lesson in physics remember, little ones.
Children:	After nine days the researcher neared the box.
Teacher:	Was the cat alive or dead?
Children:	We do not know. The box was sealed. The cat was inside the box. Breathing oxygen. Eating a sardine. Or eating poison.
Teacher:	Let me provide an answer. Schrodinger cut carefully the string and masking tape, prised apart the double folding door. He put his head into the box.
Children:	The cat had eaten the sardine and the poison,

and breathed deeply on the wonderful oxy-
gen gas. Then the cat devoured the head of
Mister Schrodinger.

Small boy: Mister Schrodo-dinger-linger.

Teacher: Now we will never know the answer to
the riddle of the mystery of the Quantum
Theory.

Girl in front row: Sir! Sir ! Ask his cleaning lady.

English Philosopher 1992

. . . with regard to your request for assistance in

resolving the problems of your existence

I can say that the discussion of

historical events would be

counter-productive

although you do

have my total

support.

A Cheap Sleazy Glasgow Porn Novel

1. They caw me the Flying Scotswoman, she said to him.

2. They caw me the go-bi-the-waw, he said.

3. She said, Do ye waant to get off at Paisley?

4. He said, Ah rememba ma Ma telt me a hunnert times, no to jump off a fast-moving train.

5. . . . here comes a train the noo.

6. . . . gauny slow doon hen?

7. See you, she says, stoap nippin ma heid.

Twa Fu Freens Frae Ayr

A Novel

Horrit an Dorrit,

Yin hoddin,

Yin doddin.

West of Scotland Haikus

ma een are gaun
thegither: Ah wish she wud
pit up some curtains.

nae, nae kiddin, Ah
wis havin a kip, a caur
rin ower ma heid.

ye're not oan pal,
ye canny gie ma brither
dug biskits tae eat.

a rammy ootside,
whit aboot? fuckin Peter
dropt the carry-oot.

ma dug is pan breid,
ma douts have fawin oot
ma pockit,
an yous waant a tap!

Green Bottles

Monday   Woke up, decided to take the day off work. Five
          minutes later remembered: I don't have a job.
Tuesday   Went to town, came home again, Betty was boil-
          ing, generally upset. What's the matter? I asked.
          She had been listening to the radio, something
          about a new supermarket with a bottle bank in

the car park. What will the neighbours think? she says.

Wednesday Betty calmed down, I went up to the loft, got down my ozone detection rod, poked it into the sky. The top of the rod starting sparking red sparks. I knew what this meant; too much hydro-carbon fossil fuel vapour in the atmosphere.

Thursday I pushed the car five miles into town, stopped at the off licence. Wendy on the counter. Get off the counter before the boss sees you, I said to her. Her knees were glistening under the spotlights or was it my eyes?

I see you wash your lower limbs with a chlorine-free non-phosphated soap, Wendy.

How is your tombo? she said, pointing to my dick.

Your language is not good, I said in reprimand.

How is your willie then? she giggled.

I gave her my order – 20 bottles of Old Tawny, 20 bottles of Vino Frizzy, 20 bottles of Grand Nerve de Figeck, 20 bottles of Bad and Worst Dry Wine, 20 bottles of My Bonny Moor Hen.

Pushed the car home. Up all night drinking. Betty fell into unconsciousness at two thirty. I regretted not buying an obscure French wine of the Normandy region – I have never been there.

Friday I pushed the car to the supermarket, bottle bank sitting in car park and it was empty, just like the radio said. I was shoving bottles through the port hole when a photographer shot me in action. Now I am a hero. 'I care for the environment' I was supposed to have said.

Saturday The neighbours threw a party in my honour. The

butcher told me 'We knew you were a work-shy git but now you have caught us on the other foot.'

Sunday | Thought long and hard about taking the butcher to the bottle bank, and shoving his head through the port hole.

Monday | Woke up, I will take the day off work, I said. Then I remembered – I do not have a job.

Tuesday | Went to town, came home and Betty was in tears. I threw the radio into the bucket.

Wednesday | Went to the off licence, rubbed an animal-fat free cream all over Wendy's thighs. She is a credit to vegetarians.

Thursday | Got rushed to hospital, hernia problems and heart attack. Doctor advised me to sell the car, or to take out the engine to make it lighter.

Friday | The butcher's business folded.

Saturday | The butcher woke up and got ready to go to work, then he remembered; he did not have any work to go to.

Sunday | The butcher's wife in tears.

Monday | The butcher called in to see Wendy. She rejected his advances.

Tuesday | The butcher offered himself as an ingredient at a pet food factory.

Wednesday | The head of quality control at the pet food factory rejected his offer because his body contained 'an excessive amount of a lipid-soluble substance, probably a pesticide . . .

Thursday | Went to town with the butcher. To save polluting the atmosphere, we pushed the car there and back.

How can I get my rocks off with Wendy? he asked me.

	You have got to charm her, I said, buy her things. Like what? he says.
	You could try a pair of foot insoles, strawberry-flavoured.
Friday	Went to the off licence with the butcher. Wendy wasn't there. She has gone to California, the boss said; they got real juicy oranges in the USA.
Saturday	Phew! The world is getting hotter, the butcher told me. Have another bottle of Bad and Worst Dry Wine, I said.
Sunday	The butcher rushed to hospital, double hernia and a heart attack.
Monday	That's it, my mind is made up – I will have to get a lighter car.

Newly Wed

a calvinistic novel
for god-fearing clean-living glaswegians

Shall we practise coitus interruptus dear? he asked.

O Yes! Let us play coitus interruptus.

What do I do? he asked, intently.

You go outside, and shut the door behind you.

. . .

What do I do now?

You wait five minutes and then knock on the door, she answered.

Cabaret Programme for the 1993 Season in the Auld Howff

JULY

Friday 29th   Dessie and Dick.
Saturday 30th Dessie, Dick and Lillie.

AUGUST

Friday 5th   Dick and Lillie.
Saturday 6th   Dessie.
Sunday 7th   Party Nite including Darts and Bingo.
Friday 12th   Tibetan Nomad Fancy Dress Nite.
Saturday 13th Dick.
Friday 17th   Family Nite with Medievil Bouncy Castle.
Saturday 18th Dick and Dessie.
Monday 20th   Elvis Presley in Concert.
Friday 24th   Lillie, Dick and Dessie.
Saturday 25th How to Build a Stone Dyke, an Outdoor Activity
                   starting at 6 am.

SEPTEMBER

Saturday 1st   Dick, Lillie and Dessie.
Sunday 2nd   Zulu Fancy Dress Nite.
Monday 3rd   Lillie.
Friday 7th   Scottish Family Nite sponsored by Minnigaff
                   TV Satellite Systems.
Saturday 8th   Dick, Dessie and Lillie.
Sunday 9th   Dick, Dessie and Surprise Guest.

Monday 10th   Secrets of Home Baking by the Creetown Obese
                         Society.
Friday 14th   .   Lillie and Dick's Farewell Party.
Saturday 15th (Private Party – Staff Only.)

Another Lesson

The creative writing teacher told her class to write a haiku.
Breize wrote: A High Coo. 'I see you live in Scotland,' said
the teacher.

– 'Yes, I do,' said Breize, 'and I have not written a haiku
although I hent poetry.' 'You kent poetry?'

– 'No.'

'Very well. What word rimes with bleed?'

– 'Gleed,' said Breize, and no fair-haired Anglo-Saxon was
in the class to disagree. 'Tonight, are you going home on the
telephage?' asked the teacher.

– 'No, I do not possess a travelling ulcer, teacher.' 'Breize!
what I should have said was – are you going home on the
telpherage?'

– 'My briefcase goes home by such means, but I prefer to go
home as a biped on a bicycle; biremes are a thing of the past.'
'I go home in a Bean,' said the teacher to Breize.

– 'The Hadfield Bean! A five-seater tourer with weather
equipment supplied.' 'How observant you are, Breize.'

– 'Did you know that vintage cars belong in the field of
chrematistics?' 'They do, do they? I park mine in a garage.'

– 'Teacher, to which family does the Etruscan language
belong?'

'Now Breize, that is a tricky one. I would say the O'Cahuns.

They live in Kilkishkeen. A language is like the cormorant. A cormorant swallows fish. He swims under water, he comes to the surface, he rests a while and then he goes under water again. Sometimes you can see a cormorant, sometimes a cormorant can not be seen.'

– 'The cormorant is like a language. A language swallows words. It swims under water, it comes to the surface, it rests a while and then it goes under water again. Sometimes you can see a language, sometimes a language can not be seen.'

West of Scotland 'Modern' Haikus

she wis a big wummin
bit she knew hir joab,
backside forrit.

> see ma caur,
> it's fawin tae pieces
> – bit Ah'm no botherin ma arse.

he telt me hissel
she's no real
– hir faimly steyed up his close.

> Glasga's great, Ah telt the Englishman,
> then the cunts nixt door
> panned oor windy in.
> Murder polis, Ah shoutit,
> an the Englishman
> said Ah wis no tae dae onything 'rash'.

ALAN WARNER

A Spot of Night Fishing
(for Kenny Crichton)

They got sent camping and were in trouble within the hour. Never seen cats-eyes in the roads before, they were digging them out with the pen knife to show the girls back in the scheme when the police car came round the corner. Gave them a lift to the farm.

Said he was the owner of the trees and they could camp if they painted his shed. When they got to it three combine harvesters were inside and the paint was a kind of tar; they could hardly get the sticks out the pots. They gave up when Moncur got attacked by the goose at the ladder-bottom.

Embarrassed cause they'd kicked the goose to death, they chucked it in the river. It caught on some weeds.

After dark they lit a bonfire by the tents. They were starving so they went for a spot of night fishing with the rod. Returned with an eel and a bucket of tadpoles. They boiled the tadpoles; when the dead ones floated to the top they ate them. The eel tasted like rabbit.

Driven by hunger, they searched the banks, hooked the dead goose and threw it on the fire. The bird burst into flames as the big bikers with some girls with bottles stepped out the dark. The bikers told them to fuck off for the night and couples got into the tents.

A steady rain was falling. They shivered under the tree. Except for Hiphearan. He'd climbed up into the dripping branches and wouldn't come down, even when first light showed on the hills.

Yonder Cunt

He's rolling the other down the stone steps, pushing him on with the toe of his boot, then the other – the rolling guy – he gets up, stumbles across the level portions of the long stairway then willingly ducks down under his companion's boot again and his rolling hulk turns over down the next run of steps till they're beside me on a level portion and the standing cunt holding the two bottles goes, 'It's a flat bit again O'Hanlon, get up and walk.'

Smears 1

I'd gone to the cash dispenser to get more cause I'd scored for sure. A car sped round a corner, its windows open and the occupants leaning from them. I was trying to make out what they were shouting when something impacted and felt wet on my sleeve.

I'd been hit by a fucking egg.

I made my way back to the late-night bar. The girl was still there. I put more drink on the table. After a while listening, I saw her look at me weird-like.

What's that on your face? she said.

I reached up. Blood was pissing from my nose. I wiped it on my sleeve and she saw all the yolk.

I got hit by an egg, I explained.

Smears 2

Back at hers we rolled off the couch. The room had polished bare floorboards and lots of little coins were jammed in the gaps between the boards, ½p and 5p bits.

Look, I said.

There was a strange shadow on her face. We'd landed on this dispenser of her boot polish and it was getting everywhere.

In daylight I stumbled around searching for the toilet but couldn't find it.

Black handprints and streaks were all along the walls.

A Good Impression
(for Murray Hunter)

I'm standing in the busy bus station where we'd to meet so's my brother could introduce me to the top man, only my best gear on to make a good impression and this dirty looking fucking wee smelly Oaktown cunt with snotters hinging is staring at me holding the crappiest little old Kodak you've ever seen so I growls, Hey cunt, are you seeing enough or what?

Can I take a photie o your trainers? he says.

What!

Can I take a photie o your trainers man, please?

A photie – what the fuck for?

Oh please mister, please, I like to draw them.

What, trainers?

Oh aye, please man – never see a pair o trainers like that up our way y'know, I gottie come down the west end to see those – please!

So here I am No. 1 hard man suppos-ed starting to go beetroot and a few cunts waiting on buses are smiling at me and my neck is doing overtime scoping that my brother and the top man are fuck all anywhere to be seen so I hiss, Well fucking get on with it. And jesus-good-god-almighty-high-cunt the embarrassing wee fuck clambers down on his tummy and elbows then starts squirming up, clawing at the camera, putting on this big flash attachment by the toes of my Nikey Huaraches and folk are laughing and shaking heads, yet I don't walk away or stamp the wee tit's head into the chuddy-stained pavement, I let him line up his shot then BOOOFF I'm blinded by the flash taking a few steps back big blobby shapes are patrolling around my vision and through it all I see the top man stood with my brother staring at me from the window of the cafe, staring at me weird as fuck.

Blood of Eden
(for P.G.)

They were arguing who was hardest that night – Hiphearan, Skiabhanach and Burdie fae Burdie.

Hiphearan took out the saw and drew it on its own weight back and forth over Skiabhanach's arm five times before Skiabhanach gave up.

Skiabhanach pulled the saw on its own weight seven times over Hiphearan's arm before Hiphearan gave up.

Burdie fae Burdie let Skiabhanach then Hiphearan draw the

saw across the skin of his arm a total of eleven times – until it reached just bone.

Then Burdie fae Burdie didn't even phone himself the ambulance until Hiphearan and Skiabhanach got their rounds in and last orders were rung.

ALISON KERMACK

Feerd

kizzy ast
firriz fare
a wee bit
too loud

kizziz ize
wur
lookn diffrint
waze

kizzy didny
wok strate
doon thi ile

kizzy lookt
it ivrywun
grinnin

ivry
singul
wunny us
stared
ooty thi windy

Uniform Feelings

jenerilly speekn
wimmin huv this thing
aboot men
in yooniforums

thay wonty
UNDRESS thum

this iz troo
ah hate that yooniforum shit
GET THUM OAFF!

Revolution

Ma handty goad itz thi trooth. Ivry nite ah take oot ma folsurz
an stick thum in thi tumblurry cleenin stuff, nexty ma bed. Ah
wotch thum spiral doon in thi wottur nsettul it thi bottum,
olwaze thi same.

Well it wiz jist thi uthur mornin, ah woke up blackn bloo.
Kidny buleev it. Ah wiz cuvurt in bite marx.

Freedom of Choice

supty yoo
yoor dissishin
whichur yi wontin
this ur that

naw yi canny huv enny thame
ah telt yi
wunny theez too
ur nuthin

whidjy meen that?
yir no wontin that
shoorly

well supty yoo
bit ahd go fur this
yir bettur oaf wi this
tellnyi

moan noo
am waitin
hurry up
make up yir mine

GORDON LEGGE

Suggestion

Listen,
whit it is is
s'posin, jist
s'posin right,
thit awis
ti pit it
yi
thit
likes,
likesih,
mean ken
mnevr   like,
no   goat a loat
goin fir mi nthat, bit,   mawfy kinna
will, will
basically
aw msane's,
nChrist kens
cuz mnae ile-paintn rthat,
bit jist   mibbee
thir's a   chance –
a chance   thit yi
kid see   yir wye
fit ti   gettn
roon   ti thinkn boot dane mi
thi great   honour ih goin nbeen ma hen.

JOHN ABERDEIN

Trystin

She wisna a hure but she needit the money, Nessie: Tomnahurich needit the company, wi a ride thrown in. Nessie hid fower or five dependents or onhingers, an hungers o hir ain: Tomnahurich, shargar-survivor, wis gaain throu life himlane.

Nessie's sister hid sellt hir a Yale tae the riverside flat, the dormer. There wis aye a beech tree shakkin its habit ootside the windae, an a commonweal o swans an gulls fleein an driftin the reaches o the river.

But fa the fuck hid een for scenery?

They wid meet antrin times, on hir day aff fae rinnin the rule on Presto's tills, file ee mebbe waitit a load till ees larry, hunnerwecht secks o saumon feed or crinkly yella coils o drainage pipin.

Tomnahurich hid a humphy-back, an Nessie wis twenty stane if she wis a day, sae aftentimes they nivver gaed pubbin first but jist slippit doon tae the flat, Ness first: she wid aye pit hir haun on ees cock as ee arrivit on the tap landin.

Tae say *Hello* like, *Foo's yir doos?*

But this day in November she wis pushed for time, Nessie, an said tae wee Tam *Ye'll jist hae tae eese ma express check-oot, ten items or less.*

The Hurich grinnt back at her *Ye'll be lucky if Ah've onythin in ma basket avaa eftir last time, cunt ye* an made a dive for hir big mammies.

*Dinna rumple ma dress, Ah've got ma auld man's fruneal at
hauf-twelve, ken?*

Ah didna ken ee wis deid. Fit the fuck did ee die o?

Fit div ye fuckin think?

Sae she sat doon on the side o the bed, twenty stane maks an
affa dent, an says *A wyce wee nipper wid see tae ma zipper.* Syne
she says *Tak the hyeuks fae ma eyes an feel the size.*

Wee Hurich got hir cuppit an himsel a wabbly hard-on, till
ower hir shouder an across the river ee clockit een on the
braid-staired kirk wi this brash new sign *Brahan & MacBrahan:
Funeral Home.*

She aye hid a joke if ee lost it tho: *Foo mony bollacks has a
horny gollach?* or *Iss is a summons, far's yir comins?*

An she parkit hirsel on hir back.

Aince Tam hid got clambert aboord an intae gear, Nessie wid
loll hir heid tae the ae side an time'm on the reid-winker o the
bed-alarm: it wis fifty pence a meenit she coinit, fifty p fan ee
wis up an revvin like, the gas wis tae pey an the twins wintit awa
on some ootdoor trippie.

Nae that it wis a yawn aathegither but ees cock made nae mair
impression on hir than a budgie crashin on Ben MacDhui.

Ee kept sayin *Ah luve ye, Ah really luve ye* an Ness wid coo back
One fifty, darlin, syne *Twa pund, ma dear,* toothin ees lug tae
mark the fiverswarths.

At's a tenner noo sma bite, the kids wintit CDs fae Sunty
Claas.

Fifteen, Tam sooky-bite, nae tae mention the cat tae the vet.

Twenty muckler bite, an ither arrears.

An sae it gaed on.

Tam wis gaain *Ah cannae see me haein an organism this side o Christmas* an gaain *Ness lass, div ye tak Access?* Ee wid be skint lang afore ee wis milkit, nae that that scunnert'm nane, fit else wis there tae splurge yir money on, noo that yir mither wis oot o the leaky highflat, slavverin awa in the guff o the Hame?

Betimes Tam wid droop, dwyne on hir breist, she wis guid till'm, she stappit coontin file ee lay like a wabbit rabbit at the door o hir fud's-burra, Tam hufflin an snufflin in hir breist an hair. Syne she wid tell'm tae gee ees ginger *Ah'm needin yir Yorkie up ma porkie.*

In the line o the makars wis Nessie richt eneuch.

Sae back up the cash-aisle went Hurich, aa in a haze wi the saft nithins in ees lug.

Forty pun fifty, humphit, humphit, *Forty-wan,* humph, humph, fan she suddentlie sterts greetin. *Ye'll hae tae fuckin hurry up, Tam. It's nae funny. Ah've bare hauf an oor till auld Jock's fruneal!*

An wi that she hurdlit a great leg ower'm sae that Tam, still up there, noo wis in fae ahint, that wid sune connach'm, hir bum braw big like twa Monadhliadh vrappit roon ees doins. Weil ee lat oot an affa sigh an raxit for the bedposts, findin nithin, she hid swung like a lock-gate slanteyweys across the sheet.

Tam wis left astarin oot the windae at a river slidin by.

Ee kneadit hir shoulders noo an lat aff the air-brakes, o she skirlt a bittie, grantit, for by this time ees baas were diddlin *Heyderrydan on yir fantanteran.* Hir heid hung doon athwart the side o the bed, saftgaitherin in hir pleasure as she eesed tae dae langsyne, lassie in the lang gress, blithe ahin the bushes.

An *O, O!* it wis fine, hir heid gaain up an doon, an erse

the mair sae, hir fud ran honey an hir heid wis bees, murrin *Tammyfu Tammyfuh Tammyfuchmefuchme* she culdna say *Fuck* ony mair, puir lass.

Sae wee Tomnahurich jist tuggit the clock fae the wa, an settlit in aboot hir, big Ness, cockswallt an prood o himsel, as throu the gless he watchit yella leaves, leaves in black swurls, furlin doon the winter river.

The Warld or Buckie

I kent a mannie aince gaithert seaweed. Nae shite aboot teethpaste extraction or trace aliments, ee jist gaithert seaweed tae clart ower the laun, mebbe tae smoor aa that dockens, or gie fuckin daffies somethin tae think aboot, a mulch tae the general. Ee haalit wi a pair o haun-shafts a hurlie wi pneumatic tyres.

Ee said it wis a faur better ambition than hoofin roon at the Olympics or be chief doofer at Westminster, acaus ye aye hid it in front o ye. Ye nivver scratchit yir baas in the mornin an thocht *Weil, that's deen. Noo fit?*

Ah stoppit'm on the road ae day, fan a bonny sun wis birslin ees back, an aa the maggots vrasslin throu ees greenbroonmash.
   The laun's exhaustit ee said. *It's needin a richt feed. We canna wait or the Sacont Flood.*
   At's richt, Noah Ah said, ye hiv tae humour them, ken?

As far as Ah mind the mannie wis fae Buckie.

The Can-Can, ken?

That winter Jock wis ower at the new incinerator, labourin, an bidin in digs in Rose Street. Ees laundlady wis a doctor's wife, a slim thing fae Paris haurdlie aulder than Jock himsel, but hubbie hid rin awa tae Saudi, leavin hir wi three snappers aroon the drum. Ivvery nicht Jock trampit hame fae the bus stop, sat doon heavy tae ees tea, an rose the lichter twa oors later acause Chantalle sat an spowk till'm. Eftir a wik, Chantalle cam intil ees bed.

A la bonne franquette said Chantalle.

Ye winna be needin that goonie, then said Jock.

Eftir twa days, Jock wisna fit, mentally, for ees wark nae mair. He bade aroon the digs, wi Chantalle's leg aye trippan'm up like a liana in a *Tarzan* film. The Fireside Rugg, the Hard Cheer, the Lobby Press, they were gey hame-made wi each ither. Only fan the kids were snoozin, like, or ben the ither room, or luikin the ither wey. Wild oats wisna in it, it wis like steerin bubblin porridge wi Chantalle, ye hidna time tae lift clear yir spurtle afore ye wid sense hir hotterin again.

Il va falloir qu'on fonce pour tout finir ce soir gasped Chantalle.

Fitivver taks yir fancy quo Jock.

Wi Jock nae warkin, an Chantalle's cheques fae Saudi dryan up, it wis time tae tak stock. Jock pushit throu the swing-doors at Presto's, plenty stock there for ony billie wi a poacher's pooch. Ee wis aa the bash: Chantalle hid shewed halfers o a lacy pillowslip inside ees donkey jeckit.

Bulk's the bugger thocht Jock. *Nivver mind the Kelloggs, Ah'll jist chore bacon.*

Chest stappt wi chocslabs, fletpackt raisins an sectors o Brie, ee rummaged aroon like Aiberdeen's answer tae an armadillo. He cam tae the cash-oot visibly throttlin a bottlie o mulk.

Is that aa yir needin? said the quine at the desk.

Pas anglais. Je prefere culbuter replied Jock.

Chantalle wis fine pleased: the kids popped raisins an slabbered the chocolate, she wis sune throu the Brie as Jock pigged intae bacon. The morn wis hir twenty-fifth, sae they hit on a plan atween them aa.

Venez: nanan she temptit the trio.

C'est du nanan she reassured Jock.

Chantalle went intae Presto's first, an lowsed the kids. Fae aa airts they cam runnin tae hir basket wi fine nyumnyums: jubjubs, bonbons, KitKats, you name it. Syne Jock cam in, flappin an Oxfam anorak sizes ower big like an Arab's burnous. Cake an caunles an twa frozen pizza ee poochit nae bother, aye but booze wis the puzzler, the shelfs weil-garrisoned, sae hence their wee plan.

La vie du chateau Chantalle hid promist.

Close bi the dear drinks Jock jist hoverit, bummin *Will Ye No Come Back Again?*

Syne Chantalle reappeared in hir bra-free Breton, trolleyin petitely up tae far a triangle o beantins stude, farts in a trance, in their high-stackt Eiffel. The aisles at Presto's are nae Champs Elysee, as aabuddy kens, an she suddentlie got hir wheel tae caa roon an caa the lot doon. It caused a bigger rummle than the show at the Moulin Rouge, cans an cans rollin aawey, wi aa the folk gowkin.

Merde alors! skirled Chantalle.

Mercy me! echoed Jock, an nickt a quick Fiddich, drappin it saftly intae ees lace-trimmed intimmers.

Glosses

A la bonne franquette:
    Without ceremony.
Ye winna be needin that goonie, then:
    In that case you may be over-dressed for the occasion.

Il va falloir qu'on fonce pour tout finir ce soir:
    We'll have to pull our finger out if we want to be finished
    by tonight.
Fitivver taks yir fancy:
    I trust to your imagination to choose a more appropriate
    technique.

Is that aa yir needin?:
    Have you no wish to purchase further groceries?
Pas Anglais. Je prefere culbuter:
    I am not an Englishspeaker. I prefer to diddle you lot / have
    a good fuck.

Venez: nanan:
    Come. Let's get some yummy-yummy.
    C'est du nanan:
    It's a piece of cake.

La vie du chateau:
    The life of the castle.
    Will Ye No Come Back Again?
    Early Drambuie jingle.

Merde alors!
    Shit, then!
    Mercy me!
    May the Lord shower grace on my head!

Concrete. Poetry.

Gray Dunn Caramel Wafers they were biggan a warehoose for, oot past the Brig o Don. A toon the size o Aiberdeen eats an affa caramel wafers. A toon the size o Aiberdeen needs somethin tae chow. An if it's nae caramel wafers it'll be lugs.

Dino walkit aa the wey oot tae ees wark. He wisna ridan naebuddy at the time. Hertsair, gey cranky in the cock, he walkit the full length o King Street, past Fire Stations, monumental masons, the roosty railwey's auld stane brig, the green-railed skweel, a thoosan granite hooses, Pittodrie, Varsity, St Machar, Seaton, ower the Bleak Brig o the Shiftin Sauns, oot the dual carriagewey an up tae ees wark.

Like fuck. He tuik the bus. Ninepence.

He warkit wi an auld German prisoner o war that had bidden on eftir tae wark in Aiberdeen. Probably nivver noticed ony differ. Ludwig, he wis caad, the nicest o the lot. He wis the ganger, an fan ee saw fit a miserable sotter Dino wis in, he lat him be tea-loon.

Ach, bide in the shed, yungling, ve manage mitout you the day.

Weil, atween fillan kettles, sweelin mugs, runnin for bridies an swypin up flaky crumbs, ony gommeril wi a spirk o sense culd mak bein tea-loon spin oot hauf the wik. Specially if ee wis listan tae keep up wi the *P&J*'s political analysis an scribble oot pomes on the back o a bridie-bug. Fae Monday tae Friday he haurdlie pit hauns in ees rubber glubs, haurdlie dampent ees wellies. Tho Dougie, Greggie an Hindoo wid aye deave at'm.

Nae comin oot tae play wi yir shuvvel the day, Dino?
Iss tea, fit hiv ye deen, pisst in't?

*Did they nae teach ye at college foo tae keep a bridie warm,
ye radge?*

Ae nicht ee did walk hame.

Neist day there wis a panic on. The Ready-Mix wis due in at
twalve an hauf the shutterin wis aa tae shite. Nae level. Start
storin caramel wafers on a slopin fleer an far will it aa end?

Steel mattin an twistit steel rod wis fleein aawey, shutterin wis
gettin battert thegither, an aabuddy wis in a fine bad humour.
Even Ludwig wis flustert.

*Dino, fesh twei nails-boxes to Aleek, he's bin klagend for dem
funf meenoots noo!*

Okay.

*Dino, queeck wi the wid for Simson, oder he says your mutter
won't know you!*

Aye, okay!

*Dino, Schmerzen und Unlust disna build nathing . . . schnell,
schnell!*

Unlust wis fit he hid, Dino, an fan the stramash wis at the ither
side, he nickt intae the sheddie, pit on the twa kettles ten meenits
early an sat ower ees pome wi a pencil.

> *In Aberdeen the granite is no facade*
> > *I feel ghostly*
> *I leave my flesh when I walk abroad*
> > *Or mostly.*
>
> *I flit across the no-man's road*
> > *Between the tall blocks float*
> *Hard to tell* ~~myself~~   ~~my soul~~   *this errant ghost*
> > *From an empty coat.*

Ootside cam the roar o the Ready-Mix arrivan, drum dirlin roon like surf tumblin on chingle. Like surf tumblin . . . like surf tumblin.

Weil the cunt'll hae tae come oot! We're nithin like ready but the cunt'll hae tae come oot!

Dino thocht they micht have been speakin aboot him, but na. There cam the soond o the hale load o Ready-Mix gushin oot like glashiers caufin in th'Antarctic. The lorry culdna bide, they wid jist hae tae barra fan they were ready, the stuffie wid sune ging aff.

Dougie, Greggie an Hindoo cam tearin in, blatterin the door.

Far's that fucker Dino?

Luik fit's happened ye bitch's twat! We're ahin wi twa ton o Ready-Mix, an ye're in here tooterin wi a pencil!

Gie's a haud o that!

And Dougie tore the boddom o Dino's bridie-bug fae ees haun. He read oot fit wis vroten. *Listen tae this shite we've got tae pit up wi*:

> Is it the coat that notes the neat steel rails
>   And rather likes their stitches
> Hemming the garden to the granite mansion
>   The Aberdonians to their niches?

Greggie said *Hem ye, ah'll fuckin hem ye!*

Get'm ootside said Hindoo.

An they tuik him, chuckin ees bridie-pome tae the nort-vind, an yarked him up on tap o the pile o Ready-Mix, haudin ees airms oot helpless till ee rugglit an sank.

Poet said Hindoo *fucking statue!*

The weet concrete cam ower ees welly-taps like lumps o

parritch. An aye the tither yilp o bree. He shooglit an scrunched ees boots up an doon but there wis nae wey oot. Even Ludwig wis lauchin. *Heh, Dino, I thocht it was aye ve Jarmans in the varst boots, heh?*

It wis like eatin caramel wafers wi yir legs.

University o Life, like

Hir hair wis fine yellach an hir een wir bluachie. Ae luik exchangit across the airy mezzanine, an ee culd've gone haund-ower-haund ower the Blondin. This wis nae cakir fae Dough Skweel nor willydazzler fae Dumf, she wis a spleet-new bejanella.

The Varsity shelvins were full wi ten million wirds, fae *Beowulf* tae *Fa's Feart o thon Woolf Wifie?* A sparra flew across the ha.

He crept up ahint hir an clappit twa hauns roon hir lambswool breists. *Guess fa?* Roon she upsprang an swung wi hir teeth in ees lower lip. *Woof-woof!*

They circled up the firebossed stair, lurkin in the *Scrutiny* stack till the Varsity jannie clickt aff an lockit the brichter wisdoms.

Dark aerobatics o hert an loin. She wis aye tae mind. Eftir she bit'm, ees moo wis reidachie.

The Odd Fish

Ardmair Bay wisna that guid ony mair. Fit did ye expeck nooadays: virgin grund? There suld be a sang *Ardmair Nae Mair* aboot the Prann across the Wattir or even the Prann that wid be King!

Wi a chorus *Aye a Prann for Cherlie* . . .

It was a simmer's Settirday mornin. Armstrong, Borders' name, hid just skybootit on the mune. *Far were ye fan they laundit on the mune? Creelin in Ardmair Bay.* The soonder wi its muvin pen wis scrollin double smudges, nae a guid sign. They muvit on.

Ye nivver shoot on the hard.

Fit wey no, Johnny?

At's feel, at. Ye winna get pranns on the hard.

Efter some haals Shagus wid leave the grizzlin wee skipper an ging ahint ees tooter of a wheelhouse, haudin ontae the crackit mast. The 30-fitter sweyed back and fore.

Ee felt grand in the boat, midgetty under Ben More, an ees jeans swalled at the thocht o the weekend.

Ye'd bettir get at next bow hyeukit. There's haurdly nae pranns last time.

Fit wey div ye aye fish here then?

It's handy for gaain in an oot Ullapool. It's aa the same onywey.

The *Regal* wis in mair at the Isle Martin side, faur the auld monastery man bade. Brither Martin wid nivver have fossickt aboot for pranns for ees brakfeest, matins syne limpets mairlike.

The boathyeuk was lang, gnarlt as ony saga. As the *Regal*

peched an slawed in a curve, Shagus cleuked up the green end, slabbert it ower the Evanton haaler, and slottit the raip in the birlin groove. Aa went ticht as a bell-raip, smooth as meditation, as the first creel muved silent tae the surface and cam clear in a glister o splashes.

Ee culd see the broon thresh of the fiddlers neukit in the boddom, the baitstrings bare. Crabs were aye hungert. Shot on the hard! Ee wis shakkin oot the dross, insertin a sliver o saut machrel, stackin the creels, ten in aa, aa wasters, their ropes trailin doon like a forfochen Medusa.

Me doos are itchy ee thocht.

Culdna mind fa had tellt him that ane but it wis true. The yella Vinco ylies didna breathe. Yir baas needit to breathe, nae aabuddy kent that. Shagus wore the kilt ashore.

Awa an pit the kettle on for wir piece.

A score o creels had yieldit nae a score of pranns, orangey-pink, schnappin their tails wi antrin bursts o conviction.

There wis an auld reid tin o Carnation, slits gone yella wi auld man's milk. Fa wis it said that, auld man's milk? A recipe wisn't it, some smert billie's name for Athole Brose? Ee made fower safties wi marge an cheddar.

Johnny, fit boat did you hae again?

O I hid the Guide Me, *me an ma breeder. We were aye at the seine, the seine-net, warkin oot a Buckie. A forty-odd year.*

Did ye like that better?

Whewff! This tea's affa het, ye tryin tae scaud ma mou?

No, Na, sorry. Jist tryin tae gie ye a heat, Johnny. Tell us, aa the years ye were at it, fit did ye like best at the fishin?

Nithin.

Nithin at aa?

Nithin avaa. Nivver ivver likit i fishin. A weet scunner.

Shagus sat tae ees wark on the gunnel, raxin their tails aff ontae the pinky-orange heap in the wicker. The boat wis rockin an Shagus felt the auld stanes o Ben More Coigach and Isle Martin takkin turns, lowerin oot ower'm, time an time aboot: mystic, monastic.

The eftirneen went a wee bit better. They saa nae boats and a cauld vind funnellt in and freshent. He got a grey dugfish in ane, lang snakeshark wi a spinstery mou. He got a grey conger in anither, durty needles o teeth, syne a beauty o a Ballan wrasse, irissy, poutin.

It was guid fun the creels, like browsin wi yir heid bent doon to the laichest shelf in the library.

An Jean wis comin up at the weekend, hir letter crumplit, aye in ees back pooch. The last creel cam up, drapit in lang broon ware. A queer jigger stuck in its riggin.

Fat-lippt, squidgy, spiky.

He thocht ee kent it, fae fan ee wis gowkin for ootlaun species, Christ splash-nettin for Tilapia, Kandinsky's mental fish. This ane wis Scottus, Cottus . . . ?

Johnny, see this ane, fit div ye ca this ane?

  Watch at spine, it'll pizen ye!

  Cottus Scorpius or somethin?

  Johnny spat oot the wheelhoose winda.

  Na, na, we aye cried it Cuntie.

Jamie o Twabuggers

Jamie o Twabuggers wis an affa loon fir neeps. Ee wid sow them, hyow them an chow them till ees hert's content. In fack ee wid hiv mairried a sweet neep, an a swede an aa, aa wimplit wi green schaws, gin ee hidna been snafflit bi Aggie Bubby first.

The couple an their mithers wir haein fancy tea in the front room, tae annoonce their engagement.

Fa wis Aggie Bubby? Aggie Bubby wis thon orra lass wi tits wallopin fae Banchory tae Bennachie, a shock o hair like a birk wid, an a fuckin quim bi aa accoont that ye culd row backanforein like a ro-ro ferry. Affa pleasant spoken.

Jamie, ye daud o shite, get yir moo aff that neep, an gie ma bubbies a richt sook, they're like a rummle o hedgehogs tae mi.

Aa this eftir she'd cowpit'm doon on the fleer ahin the settee.

Jamie, stap sookin ma tit in that mim-mou'd kinna wey ye silly radge. Ma cunt's needin dirlin.

Aa this eftir she'd splattert ees neep tae the skirtin an haaled ees spaver open-shive.

Jamie, Ah tellt ye tae pit yir cock in ma fud, nae yir pinkie finger: stap playin wi the foal's mane an gie's a fuckin ride.

Syne auld Mrs Twabuggers an auld Mrs Bubby, comin up as smooth as twa munes ower the antimacassers, gied their loon an quine pelters wi eclairs an meringues.

DUNCAN McLEAN

Own Words

There were four of us lifted for questioning. In your own words, they began, Tell us what you were up to.

    . . . . . . said Ally.

    Bor stiggle zoxon, said Bud.

    Fuck off filth, said Col.

    They had a quick confab, then turned to me. In *our* own words, they asked, What was going on?

    Soon they had all they wanted.

II

CLOCKTOWER
PRESS

ahead of its time

JAMES MEEK

Bonny Boat Speed

When I see Arnold I remember the woman who could walk. I think about Jenny too of course, not that she looked anything like her dad. I haven't seen her for a long time now. That was why I stopped the woman who could walk, to find out when the healing would be over and Jenny would come out. I didn't go inside. I had nothing that needed healing then. Nothing that you would stand up and say you believed in Jesus for, or that you'd know if you'd been healed of. Praise the Lord! I can love the ones I didn't love before, and stopped loving the ones that didn't love me! Hallelulia! I walked up to the hall entrance slowly, early, and I was reading the curved red letters on freshpasted white paper about Pastor Samuel's Ark of Salvation when the woman who could walk walked out. I knew she could walk because she told me. She was big and mobile in skirt and sweater and her hands stuck in the pockets of her open raincoat which was flying behind her in the warm wind over the car park, her face was white and her mouth slightly open and she was staring straight ahead. She had a crutch tucked under her right arm. I had to catch her by the elbow to stop her.

Excuse me, d'you know how much longer it's going on? I said.

She stopped, one foot lifted, balanced by my hand resting on her elbow – it was a soft, round elbow – and looked at me long enough to say: I can walk! before she walked, then ran, to her car and drove away. It was a straight slip road to the

M8, a busy enough evening with no roadworks, and as far as I could understand from the paper next morning it happened within a couple of minutes of her merging with the flow that the juggernaut swung easily through the barriers and hit her car head on, with a combined speed of 150 miles per hour. I suppose Pastor Samuel might have said Well, I healed her, so the least she could've done was to have stayed to the end of the meeting. Now she walks, nay drives, with the Lord.

I was concerned for myself. I kept her back for half a second and the juggernaut hit her. In half a second a truck travelling at 70 miles an hour travels its own length twice – that's what Arnold told me when I shared this with him, a free sample. From her side she could have avoided the truck by being more polite. We were both in the wrong. I suffered by not knowing I'd have to wait quarter of an hour for Jenny to come out. The woman who could walk suffered by being conscious for at least 30 seconds of the sensation of the destruction of her body by an oncoming lorry (spontaneous Arnoldism). Usually when I think about the woman who walked the thought is: I didn't summon up the juggernaut, did I. You don't guess the instant when northbound and southbound collide, like a single bolt of lightning. Only when I see Arnold I think about how maybe everything is equalled out in the end, not in a good way, and how easy it is to summon up an irresistible opposing force, after all.

What Siobhan said this one time, and the tenner pointing at my empty tumbler was sharp and fresh as a new razor, was even more ominous than Arnold lurking round the pub as he was: Same one again? she said. Not Same again? but Same one again?

Ah, better not, last ferry and all. I looked down into the glass and dodgemed the sleek humps of ice around the bottom. The unnecessary One hung in the air.

Go on, said Siobhan. You sold a house today, didn't you? Take a cab.

I sell a house most days. I sold one yesterday.

It was a big one, you said.

It was a big one. I felt like rewarding myself with a third g & t. But the taxis skin you for a ferry trip and it's no better picking up a second one on the other side.

I can't drive after three, I said.

Take a cab. Two gin and tonics please, she said. She'd seen the weakness in my face and got the order out the way so we could argue about it over a drink.

I don't want to take a cab, I said, looking over at Arnold sitting by himself at the table by the cigarette machine. He was working, he had the yellow pad out in front of him. He turned and smiled at me. I looked at Siobhan.

It's not the money, I said. I don't like being screwed. I've got to take the car across. I've got a season ticket.

Well drive then, she said, holding the two glasses out in front of her.

But I can't if I have a third drink, I said. I took one of the glasses from her.

Don't drink it, she said.

I won't, I said, and took a mouthful of the stuff and swallowed it down.

You're so weak, she said, smiling and touching her earring.

You make it sound as if that's good.

Oh, I love weak men.

So how do I get home?

I'll give you a lift back.

I was very happy. It was easy to make me happy. Maybe I'd have four drinks and all in Siobhan's company, and a free ride all the way to Kirkcaldy on the big white ship. There'd be time for one on the moon deck bar on the way over and we could sit there studying the constellations, talking. I was grinning too much too close into Siobhan's heroic delighted face and turned again to Arnold. We smiled at each other and waved, I raised my glass to him. He raised his. It looked like water.

Great, I said to Siobhan. In the rush of it I almost said I love you, not meaning it like that, but instead said: Why did you say Same one again?

Confusion sluiced darkly into her face.

You said Same one again instead of Same again.

Did I?

Yes.

She looked into the middle distance, frowning, quiet for a while. So what? she said eventually.

I took a deep drink and went under, groping for something good.

We're like sister and brother, you and me, I said.

She looked at me without saying anything for a few seconds, then put her drink in my free hand. Arnold'll give you a lift, she said, and walked out the door.

I finished my gin, sat on a bar stool and started in on hers, raising the side without lipstick to my mouth, turning it to the side with lipstick. It tasted pretty much the same. I was watching Arnold. He was scribbling away with a pencil. The bar was full but the only person I knew was Arnold, sober as an ayatollah and his car parked outside.

Once there was a group of merchants who returned to the borders of the empire after months spent crossing the great wilderness. Everyone wanted to know what it had been like. Och, it was all right, the merchants said. Hot deserts of course, cold mountains, wet jungle – still, we made it.

Folk listened to them politely, clapped them on the back and drifted back to their affairs. Some time later another group of merchants arrived. The locals gathered round – what was it like?

Incredible, the merchants answered. Absolutely unbelievable. It was so hot that the beaks of the vultures would soften and fuse together and they would die of starvation if they were careless enough to close them. It was so cold that we had to breathe on each other's eyes every five minutes to stop our eyeballs freezing solid. It was so wet that a cup held out would fill with rain faster than a man could drink it.

A huge crowd gathered round the second group of merchants, stood them drinks for a year, offered them their daughters in marriage and secured them pensions for life.

Arnold was making a good living on the discovery that folk hungered after apocryphal facts like drinkers hunger after salty snacks. He had a name. The editors would ring him up: Death Valley, Arn, they'd say, give me ten by six. And he'd sit around and write: In Death Valley in August, you can toss an ice cube in the air and it will have melted before you can catch it. Nine more like that. Or: Dead composers this week mate, say a dozen. And he'd write: If the Italian composer Vivaldi was alive, he would be the richest man on the planet, earning an estimated £1 million a minute from royalties on the use of *The Four Seasons* on telephone switchboards. The secret lay in the utter lack of research and confidence that anyone who could be bothered to challenge his published facts would be rejected as a nitpicking wanker. Besides, whenever one of his jobs appeared, it was so quickly plagiarised that it immediately took on the veracity of gospel – more so, in fact, since every second of every day somewhere in the world an average of 6.5 people challenge the authenticity of the New Testament (6.5 – what Arnold calls the precision principle in successful apocrypha) whereas no one, not even the Vatican, had ever taken the trouble to complain about Arnold's assertion that, for liturgical reasons, the Pope never flies in aircraft that can land on water.

He never said but I reckon it was something about the six

months he did for dangerous driving that got him on the apocrypha thing. He'd been terrified of getting beaten up or abused or whatever in jail and tried to keep in with the authorities on both sides by writing pornographic stories to order. And maybe after a while the sex fantasies began to fray and it began to show that there was a hunger for something else, tiny legends of a world outside, and he began to slip them in: that it wasn't just the smooth slender bodies twining over the sheet which got the screws and lifers going but the insistence in parenthesis that the ancient Egyptians had abandoned goat-hair duvets for duck-down ones when they discovered the aphrodisiac qualities of the now extinct Nilotic eider.

Almost everyone had been amazed he got sent down, he was so middle class, even the advocate was embarrassed, he hurried away afterwards and didn't speak to anyone. I wasn't surprised, though. Arnold was a dangerous driver. He's a dangerous driver now. Whatever they did to him in prison, it didn't change his overtaking habits. It was a gamble on a blind summit and he lost, collided with a car full of students from England. He killed two of them. Arnold went into an airbag but his wife in the passenger seat didn't have one. She wasn't wearing a seatbelt. Perhaps she'd been as unhappy as that. I don't know. Anyway she went through the windscreen head-first. Straight away you imagine it happening in slow motion but it doesn't, of course, you don't see it like that any more than you see the flight of a shell from a gun. There's a loud noise and in an instant, like a badly edited film, it jumps, it's all arranged across the road, perfectly, peacefully, the broken cars, the glass, the bodies and the wheels spinning slowly.

Arnold was 36, same as me. His wife died about the time my divorce came through. Since the trial he'd seen even less of Jenny than I had. She didn't think he'd killed her deliberately, no one did. Before the accident Jenny said she liked the way he drove. Afterwards she didn't hate him: nothing so passionate. She went off him. She'd just started at art college and got a flat and never went round to see him any more, in jail or out. When they paroled him I expected him to take to drink, I don't know why. He went teetotal and as soon as he got his licence back he was driving worse than before. That's to say he was a good driver, very skillful, but always found a way to drive that was out beyond the edges of his skill and relied on luck to fill the space between.

I'd left my watch at home. The clock above the bar said 10.25 and the last boat was at 11. Someone'd told me that the landlord always set the clock ten minutes fast, so that left a good three quarters of an hour to get to Queensferry. You couldn't rely on Arnold to use that time well, though. Of course everyone ran the risk that they might die on their way home from the pub. A loose slate might fall on their heads, or they might have a heart attack, get stabbed. What else could happen? There could be an earthquake. A predator could escape from the zoo. A predator could escape from his mates. But the chances were infinitesimal. It wasn't something you thought about: Better watch on my way home from the pub in case I get killed. Driving with Arnold it was. Even if the chances of death doubled at the third decimal place, you wouldn't put money on it, there was only one life. To have four gin and tonics and then go out the door thinking and now, perhaps, the afterlife, now, even before morning.

Arnold was coming over. Need a lift? he said.

No thanks.

He nodded at the door. I don't think Siobhan's coming back. Did you say something?

Yes.

Arnold jiggled his car keys. Last boat at 11, he said.

I'll get a cab.

Come on.

No really Arnie, it's great of you, I appreciate it, but I'm fine, I'm doing all right, taxis are good, they're cheap, they're reliable, they're fast. Fast enough, I mean. Not too – yeah, fast enough. Don't want to have you going out of your way.

He looked hurt. He fidgeted with his keys and looked around. He did seem astoundingly calm and sober for an Edinburgh pub on a Friday night. Con, he said, I don't understand you. We've been drinking in this place for the past two years and we both know where we go at closing time. It's not like we're strangers. What is the deal with these taxis? D'you not get embarrassed when you're getting out of the cab on the quayside and you see me driving up the ramp? D'you think I avoid the moon bar on a Friday night cause I like the Stoker's Lounge better?

I had wondered about that. My face went the colour of the carpet in the Stoker's Lounge. It'd been stupid to think he hadn't noticed me trying to avoid him on the boat all this time.

I'm sorry, Arnie, I said. I don't like the way you drive.

I hadn't meant to say that. Anyway, he was alive, was he not?

I know, said Arnold. But I'm more careful now.

No you're not. I've seen the way you go down the Queensferry Road.

That's just the way it looks. That is me being careful. I don't hit anything. I never hit anything. I make sure now. I've made sure ever since that time. It's a science, it's dynamics. Anyway, there's plenty of time, there's no need to hurry.

The clock said 10.35, i.e. 10.25, so he was right, there was plenty of time. And even though I'd seen him shoot past and slot his car at 60 through a space you wouldn't try to park in, I'd never actually driven with him.

If you're so worried about the taxi, said Arnold, you can give me a fiver if you like. He grinned.

A fiver? To Queensferry? I could get to Inverness on a fiver.

And still have money left over for a deep fried Brie supper and a chilled Vimto.

Make it ten then.

We went out to the car. We hadn't got there before he'd hit me with some new apocrypha which might've made me change my mind if I hadn't been thinking along the same lines, so much that I was hardly aware he'd said it.

The dice you'd need to roll to reflect the chances of your being involved in a car accident on any one trip, he said, would have so many faces that without a powerful microscope it would be indistinguishable from a perfect sphere.

What was that? I said, fastening the seatbelt. He repeated it while he started the car.

Bet you didn't sell that to News International, I said.

No, I just thought of that one. It's not for sale.

Private apocrypha, eh.

He didn't say anything. That didn't bother me because I was looking at the digital clock on his dashboard. We were out on the road and moving. Arnold was driving at just under the speed limit in built-up areas. Cars were passing us. The clock said 10.35.

Your clock's wrong, I said.

I know, he said.

Right.

They were going to change the name to Kingsferry, said Arnold. In honour of the king who died falling off the cliff, you know, trying to catch the boat late at night.

That's not such a good one, Arnie. Don't think you'd get far with that.

It's true! I'm off work now. No apocrypha in my free time. It's true.

Why would they call it Kingsferry? They didn't start calling Dallas Dead Presidentville after Kennedy got shot there.

Because that's what it's about. It's not about folk crossing the river.

It is as far as I'm concerned. They could call them South Ferry Ferry and North Ferry Ferry and that'd make sense to me.

No, Con, said Arnold, turning to look at me, and even though we were still trundling along at 30, I wanted him to turn back and keep his eyes on the road. He looked worried for me, as if I was about to go out alone into the world without the things I needed to know to survive. If it was about folk crossing the river there'd be a bridge. A Forth road bridge. They could easily build one. It'd be open round the clock and no one would ever have to be racing to get the last boat again.

We're not racing, though, cause we've got plenty of time.

OK, but folk do. And they're supposed to be all into public safety. I tell you what it is, it's put there deliberately. It's a deliberate exception. Because they know you can't resist it. You want it. You want a place in the country where you can be provoked into taking a risk without going out and looking for it too hard.

No you don't.

You do, Con. You know you do. There just aren't enough real risks on the go, and you don't want to go rock climbing or bungee jumping or kayaking, cause you're getting on, and it's too much trouble, and they take all the risk out of it anyway, it's like a fairground ride, and you don't want to go out looking for a fight, and violence in the pictures is just a wank . . . so you sit in the pub and you wait until you're about to miss the ferry.

Don't talk this way, Arnie, it's not good.

It's not that you want to die. You want to live. More than anything, you want to live, you want to have even just the next five minutes of your life, never mind seeing the sun come up again. Only there's something that comes in between wanting one and wanting the other, it's like a separation, you start believing two different things at the same time, that if you die, it'd be the end, and that you can die without actually dying. That you can watch it. That you can do it again. That it'd be interesting. You really believe that. It's strange. I don't understand it. D'you understand it?

A horn opened up behind us and headlights flared through the rear windscreen. The car behind pulled out sharply and overtook with a roar of contempt. Our speed had dropped to 25. So far the only way we were going to die tonight was getting spannered by a fellow motorist. I wanted to talk about going faster. I wanted to talk about what happened to Arnold's wife. I didn't want to upset him.

I'm not into the risk, I said. I was really wanting to get a lift with Siobhan and sit with her in the moon deck bar in the big white ship and go home.

Arnold didn't say anything. I hadn't thought it was possible to drive any slower in high gear but it seemed we were slipping back to about bicycle pace. I remembered he'd been after Siobhan just after he'd got out, and I remembered he'd been sitting down there in the yeasty fug of the Stoker's Lounge for two years while we'd been up there watching the lights of passing ships through the rain on the glass roof and the moon wax and wane over the flint-coloured water of the firth.

We passed the Kwik-Fit garage. I turned round to check the time on the digital clock they had.

Arnie, I said. Let's talk about time.

Despite his mastery of the laws of space and time, said Arnold, Albert Einstein never owned a watch and relied on friends to tell him what year it was.

When we left the pub it was 10.25 by the clock, I said, which was ten minutes fast, so it was 10.15. Your clock said 10.35, but you agreed that was wrong.

Stonehenge tells the time more accurately than the most sophisticated atomic clock.

The Kwik-Fit clock we've just passed says 10.50.

The landlord of the Faulkner Arms always sets his clock 10 minutes fast to make sure none of his customers misses the last boat to Fife.

Christ, was it you told me that?

I didn't think you'd believe that one, said Arnold. He's a landlord, isn't he? His clock's slow. So's mine.

I looked around. Accurate timekeeping by: Kwik-Fit. Arnold's car had central locking, controlled from the driver's seat. Traffic was shooting past. I had the impression we were standing still. But we must have been going at least as fast as a strong freestyle swimmer. Ten minutes to cover seven miles. Not at this rate. Siobhan would be on board already. She was great but it upset her that all I wanted to do was talk to her and loiter in her presence for as long as she happened to be around. She wanted love, or sex, or both, I wasn't sure, which made it strange she'd put up with me for so long. One time we did come across Arnold on the big white ship, just when Siobhan was crying over something I'd said. There are people who treat crying as like sighing or yawning but I hate it, it's a catastrophe. Once when I was wee there was a primary school trip to the city reservoir and we were walking along the foot of the dam wall and I saw some drops of water dribbling down the concrete by my head and I screamed to the teacher that the dam was about to burst. Everyone laughed and the teacher, who never missed an opportunity for a bit of child-battering, gave me a thump on the back of the head. I was relieved. I really had thought the dam was going to burst. What got me wasn't so much the thought of all of us and Mrs Swynton getting swept away by a wall of water but the chest-hollowing innocence of the first little driblets, the inadequacy of the warning they were of the thousands of tons of dark, cold, merciless water pressing against the concrete. They did warn you, but they told you nothing of how deep and overwhelming their source was. I hadn't cried since I was a boy. That was something I could have asked Pastor Samuel about.

Arnold had tried to comfort her. It'd been terrible. She kept coming up against not liking him as much as she felt she should and he kept coming up against the fucking apocrypha every time something more than inane pleasantries were called for. He hadn't been like that before. When I heard him telling her, instead of not to pay any attention to the crap I'd said, that 60 per cent of single women in their thirties were in stable relationships by the time they were forty, the thought of him scribbling away about fantasy women in his cell, struggling to meet some deadline for fear he'd get his head kicked in, and getting infected with the spores of instant harmless wee fictions for instant meaningless wee rewards, almost set me going without the pastor's help.

We were quiet up to the city boundary, him crawling along, leaning back in the seat, one hand on the wheel, ignoring the cars overtaking us, staring ahead, placid and blinking, and me trying to work out how to open the door, the effect on the fabric of the jacket of rolling and skidding for a few yards, the effect on the fabric of me, the result of grabbing the handbrake and pulling it sharply upwards, calculations of time, distance and speed, and what about going by Kincardine, a place of great and famous beauty by night.

The moment the dual carriageway came in sight Arnold stamped on the accelerator and we were away. We had five minutes to get to the terminal. Once we were up to 90, I started to think we'd make it. By the time the needle shook on 110, I was thinking we wouldn't.

We'll just fly across, then, I said.

Arnold didn't say anything. We came up behind a Mercedes dawdling along in the fast lane at 80 or so. With two sharp movements of the wheel, we slid into the slow lane and back again in front of the Merc, missing a rusting hatchback by the thickness of paintwork.

Don't do this, Arnie, I said. It's not important. Slow down. We'll get there.

I thought you liked it, said Arnold. Just to see what happens.

I never did anything to give you that idea.

You fucked my daughter without wearing a condom, said Arnold.

People get older suddenly. It builds up and comes breaking through. One instant the age you've been for years, the next, the age you'll be for years to come. A dream one night, a drink, a cloud crossing the sun, a word, a thought, and you lurch backward into the next age like a drunk going over the balcony. I felt as if I'd been seized by eight relentless hands and had clingfilm pressed down over my face and body and I couldn't fight it, it was becoming part of me and that was me for the rest of my life with this extra, unwanted, itching skin.

As things stood the rest of my life was being measured out in red cat's eyes beaded along the A90, and the vision of the long cat of after dark expired at the water's edge, if not sooner. Arnold, I said, Arnie, wait, OK. Whatever you think, let's talk. Let's take time to talk. We'll go down the waterfront and get a carryout and sit up all night and talk it over. All weekend if you want. I can't talk when you're driving like this. It's putting the wind up me.

Arnold laughed. Putting the wind up you! he said. Good. Scientists say thirty per cent of the human brain is set aside exclusively to react to fear.

Bollocks, I said. Sixty.

The laugh went out of Arnold's face. He was leaning forward, his chin almost over the wheel, staring ahead. I don't know I want you to talk, he said.

Come on Arnie. She was 17, she knew what she was doing.

She was 16.

OK, she was 16 at the beginning, but she was very self-possessed.

It's interesting you talk about possession, said Arnold.

Christ, you're the one who was doing the my daughter my daughter bit! I was working up an anger because I could see we were going to make it to the terminal and up the ramp no bother. She was old enough to be living by herself. It's not like I was the first.

Arnold's left hand came swinging off the wheel and I flinched. But he was just changing down from fifth to fourth.

What are you doing? I said. We swung off the dual carriageway onto the back road into Queensferry, the long way round to the terminal, narrower, slower, and with great opportunities for head-on collisions.

You're such a bastard, Con, said Arnold, and you never bother to remind yourself of it.

I had a tight hold of the door-grip with one hand and my seatbelt with the other. We came up behind a Capri tanking along at 70 and Arnie took it on a blind bend just as something bright and screaming came round in the other direction. I closed my eyes, bent down and wrapped my arms around my head. There was a shrieking sound and horns, the Capri must have melted its brake pads to let us in, and we lived to fight another second.

Whatever it is I've done to upset you, Arnold, I'm sorry, I shouted.

No need to shout, said Arnold, frowning.

Slow down. There's a bend – Jesus.

How d'you think it feels when your wife's just died and they put you in jail for it and the daughter you raised for sixteen years stops seeing you cause she's getting screwed by a man the same age as you are?

Not good. Bad. There's a fffffff . . . there was no connection! She didn't want to see you any more. Nothing to do with me. We were in love for a while, it was good for both of us, and then we drifted apart.

We were accelerating into absolute darkness on the wrong side of the road. There was nothing to overtake any more. Like the wrong side was smoother. I could see the orange glow of Queensferry ahead and a pale scimitar of headlights rising and falling through the trees before we got there, the car we were about to go head to head with, though we knew it, and they didn't, they'd dip their headlights and slow down a little, voodoo steps to safety, they would never know. Apart from the apocryphal 30 seconds. He'd almost convinced me with that one.

There's a car coming, I said.

It's OK. We won't hit it. You know, Con, 95 per cent of teenage girls who have relationships with men twice their age or more say love was never a factor.

I remembered reading that in *Marie Claire* when I was still seeing Jenny and worrying about it.

You're talking shite, Arnold, I said. You're starting to believe your own apocrypha. There aren't any facts about love. Would you move to the right side of the fucking road?

It was over before I had time to wet myself, and when we'd swung round the bend into the blaring glaring squealing ton of glass and metal and flesh hurtling towards us, and there'd been no contact, I realised he'd done this before. Everyone else would swerve at the last moment, at exactly the same time as the other car, but he kept on on the wrong side, letting the other car swerve, so we missed.

Stop, I said. I'm sorry. You're right and I'm wrong. I repent. Could you stop the car? I meant it. I would have knelt in the Stoker's Lounge all the way across with my lips pressed to his ringpiece just to be out in the open and not moving. It was 10.59 by his clock, we were just coming down the hill to Queensferry, and I knew he'd try to clear the High Street narrows and all the rest in 59 seconds.

You're not making any sense, Con, said Arnie. You know better than I do what incidental risk's all about, the danger that comes with getting where you want to go when you can't wait. When you were screwing Jenny it was the hell with the crash, maybe you will, maybe you won't. What's the difference? You know you crashed. You do know, don't you? You couldn't stop yourself. You knew you might, and you did. You knew a kid would only be trouble for her and she didn't want one.

I'm not with you. Just stop, eh. Stop. Stop.

I'm not intending to stop. It's hard to stop when you're almost there. You didn't stop. And there are some accidents Pastor Samuel couldn't help her with. He threw up his healing hands and said: If you don't want his child, girl, cast it out.

STOP!

And she did cast it out. Six weeks gone. She really didn't tell you, did she?

I pulled hard on the handbrake. We both went quiet for what seemed like a long time, watching the masts of the yachts fly past, like little children watching a conjuror, it seems to me with our hands folded across our laps, but I suppose not. For a certain time, memory, the present and apocrypha became the same thing, a trinity, like the Father, the Son and the Holy Ghost. I remembered the car flying off the end of the pier before it actually happened, and I felt it skim three times across the waves like a stone as if it really did, though I knew I was feeling, with every bone and muscle, the apocryphal version of what truly took place, and the vague, imaginary sense of hitting the water once and going down was what was real.

Arnie had the sunroof open and was out of it before the top of the car sank below the water. He braced his legs on the roof and plunged his arms down for me through the flood that was beating me down into the seat and tied to pull me out, forgetting about the seatbelt. We went down into the black firth together, me struggling with the belt and gulping down a gallon of salt water before I shut my mouth, him clinging on to the edges of the sunroof with one hand and tugging on my jacket shoulder with the other. I got free just as a part of me I never knew I had started to try to rationalise the death experience into something negotiable but only making it worse. We were trying to kick off our shoes and jackets and our faces were in the air. We were treading water. The ferry was steaming out of harbour a few hundred yards away. It whistled. Arnold was swimming away from me towards the pier with strong breast strokes. I paddled my feet and coughed. I hate it when folk cry. It's never good, and when it's someone you thought you were fond of, like yourself, it's a disaster. It was too late anyway. There was too much water all around. There was so much of it.

SHUG HANLAN

A Murder Witness

Brady wiz hit across the heid
wae a golf club
or if it wiznae the heid
it wiz the tap of the back
or thereaboots.

The upper half of the body
definately.

Metal woods, golfers call them,
the end bits made of metal
no wood.

A metal wood,
swung one handed.
The left hand,
there wurnae a great deal of force in it.

It could huv been onaybody
their aw golfers
ah ken its a big hobby in that scheme.

Mountain Bikes & Automobiles

A car at the UCI aboot 3 weeks ago.
It was an Escort, an auld yin.
I heard later that the police were there afterwards.
Something else
aboot the guy being handicapped.

It was in the evening,
I tanned the window with a spark plug
took a red nylon jacket.
It was crap so I threw it away.

A car going down to the shows at Musselburgh.
I was oot ma heid when I done it.
I smashed the tailgate window
and took something oot.
I canny remember whit it wiz
but it wiz a load of shite so I threw it away.

At Magdalene
jist doon from the dead end bollards
on the right hand side.
The boy probably kens it was me.

I took a red leather jacket
oot of a Volvo at B&Q aboot 3 weeks ago.
I sold it.

Along Seaview
I done a Yellow Micra
and took a silk shirt, short sleeved.
Other stuff tae,
a camera, an umbrella, and some other stupid stuff.

I wiz oot ma heid that night.
I chucked maist of it away.

A Peugeot in Northfield . . .
I'm thinking hard
trying to remember other wans
but it's hard.

Bikes. Mountain Bikes,
I've had a couple of them.
Wan in Magdalene
ootside a chippie, a wee boy's bike.
I sold it for £15.

Another wan I took frae Forbouys
beside the bank in Craigentiny.
I dont know whit make it wiz
but it had a really uncomfortable seat.
My arse was killing me
when I had to cycle it away.

That's the lot.
I've done mair I ken that
but I'm really oot ma face sometimes.
I've woken up in the cells before
and had to have the polis tell me whit I've done.

That's the truth.
Sometimes, especially wi' the norries
I canny remember anything at all.
It's miles worse than the drink.

A Concerned Uncle

I've touched her bottom,
but she had her clothes on.
She jumped on my back
and I put my hands round her
to hold her up.
That's all that happened
as far as I'm concerned.

Toast

I think it was Saturday morning
we were alone in the flat.
She told me to take my jeans off.
I was frightened so I did.

Then she told me to wank over a catalogue
and when I came
I was to put it in a cup.
I did this and during it
she was prodding me with a baseball bat.

She then put my spunk
onto a piece of toast
and tried to make me eat it.
I didn't eat it though.

Up On the Roof

Rab minds the last time he was oot on a job wi me. Willie Lows in New Craighall. We scooshed the alarm box 3 days before we actually tried to get in. We went back every night trying oot different ways and checking that the foam never came leaking through the alarm box.

Finally we jist cut the wires and waited for half an hour to see if plod arrived or if it came over their radio. I had a scanner and wis listening tae all the channels they use in the toon. I've heard they're thinkin aboot using vodaphones but till then anyone that goes oot on a job without a scanner is just being silly. Wance we got the all clear we done the padlock on the shutters, done the internal doors and got the cash oot of a cupboard.

Back then Rab's wife worried where the fuck he was goin' every night. Noo she disnae bother so much. They had arguments and he left the hoose. I think he wants to go back to her, to stay. But she disnae want him back, she wants to stay separated.

So noo he's here, lying next to me, on the roof of the Shopping Centre. Rab turns over ontae his back and looks up at the stars. We'd been smokin' afore the job so I wis expectin' him tae come away wae something cosmic.

– That slut's after every gadgee she can find.

I didnae fancy a night jist listening tae Rab slagging his wife so I got him ontae his other pet hate. – Wid she even shag the Postie?

A few years back Rab had got a job as a Xmas casual wae the GPO. Alang wae a gang of students he worked night shift at Waterloo Place, sorting letters and all that shite. Regular posties call that time of year the Pressure. Whit did they cunts know aboot pressure? It's when I'm no under pressure that I crack up.

When I'm walking hame frae the pub pished and I just decide tae dae a hoose.

Anyway, wan night the gaffer pulled Rab up and telt him they'd made a mistake, that he never should have been started. Must have got wind of his previous. He's hated Posties ever since. He likes my stories aboot daein' Post Offices. All you've got tae do is force the backdoor open, you ken that you're alright as long as you dinae touch the safe cos its the only thing that's alarmed. Then grab a couple of grand in stamps, phone cards and that sort of stuff cos we've got a guy who takes them off us.

– It's no as if she's a good ride.

I'd hud enough. We lifted the manhole covers and cut the whole fuckin lot of the wires to the shops. The Plods came and we lay there waiting no saying a word. After a while I heard them saying on the radio something aboot – We'll put it down to a fault in the system. We're standing down. It wid be the last time I ever asked Rab tae come on a job wae me. Nae wonder his wife telt him to take a hike. I left him lying there, came doon off the roof, and went in and done it.

Charged

To the first charge he replied
THAT'S A LOAD OF SHITE.
To the second charge he replied
THAT'S A LOAD OF SHITE AS WELL.
To the third charge he replied
WAKE ME UP BEFORE I GO TAE THE CELLS.
To the fourth charge he replied

TWO ROLLS AND A CUP OF TEA YA CUNT.
To the fifth charge he made no reply.

The Song That Started In The Middle Of The Bus

A long, long time ago, folk were allowed to bring drink to the game. And at that time a busload of folk went to Hampden Park to see Scotland vs. England.

The folk who sat in the front of the bus were usually old or young folk. The old folk who sat in the front of the bus kept quiet and watched that the driver went the quickest way to the game. They sometimes read papers and spoke of a time, even longer ago, when folk brought lots and lots of drink to the game. The young folk who sat in the front of the bus stared out the bus window and prayed that Scotland would beat England.

The folk who sat in the middle of the bus talked mostly among themselves. They talked about working overtime and how rare it was for their wives to want to feel their cocks in their mouths. Sometimes the folk who sat in the middle of the bus would talk to the folk who sat in the front of the bus. They would ask,

– Is this driver going the quickest way to the game?

The folk who sat in the back of the bus drank the most and started fights before and after the game. They also started off the singing in the bus. The folk in the back of the bus would start a song, then the folk who sat in the middle of the bus would join in, then the old and young folk who sat in the front of the bus would join in too.

This time a strange thing happened. A song started in the middle of the bus. The words of the song were:

THE QUEEN'S A COW
PRINCESS ANNE IS A BOOT
CHARLIE'S A POOF
MARGARET THATCHER'S A PROSTITUTE

The song was so good that all the folk who sat in the bus joined in. Even the driver joined in the song that started in the middle of the bus. Normally he just went the quickest way to the game, watched all the folk get off the bus, then sat parked in the Mount Florida area of Hampden. Sometimes he'd get comfy by stretching out on the long seat at the very back of the bus. He'd dream of singing, maybe even starting off the singing at a Scotland vs. England game.

All the folk who sat in the bus sang the song that started in the middle of the bus all the way to Hampden. And after Scotland had lost the game they sang the song that started in the middle of the bus all the way home.

On the Monday night after the game, one of the old folk who sat in the front of the bus was playing dominoes in the Masonic Club. He had his opponent on the ropes, chapping to 5s and 2s. Then he lost his concentration and began thinking about the song that started in the middle of the bus. Before he could stop himself he began to sing,

THE QUEEN'S A COW

All the other folk in the Masonic Club glared at him. His opponent protested about speech play and claimed the domino game. At the end of the week one of the old folk who sat in the front of the bus received a letter telling him he was dropped from the domino team and barred for life from the Masonic Club.

Earlier that afternoon, one of the young folk who sat in

the front of the bus was staring out of the window of his History classroom. He was replaying Scotland vs. England and wondering why God hadn't answered his prayers. The words of the lesson on the Stuart family made no impression on him. He began thinking about the song that started in the middle of the bus. Before he could stop himself he began to sing,

THE QUEEN'S A COW

Unfortunately for him the teacher was standing beside his desk and asked him to repeat what he'd just said so that the rest of the class could hear. One of the young folk who sat in the front of the bus's report card for that year read, Shows only a crude understanding of Scottish history.

To make up for the overtime he'd missed out on by going to the Scotland vs. England game, one of the folk who sat in the middle of the bus had worked late a couple of hours. When he returned home his wife was very angry. She said that they hardly saw each other nowadays and asked him if he was having an affair with another woman. His wife's accusations made no sense to him. He began thinking about the song that started in the middle of the bus. Before he could stop himself he began to sing,

PRINCESS ANNE IS A BOOT

In desperation, his wife took what he said to be a compliment. She had never heard him be so unkind to another woman before, except of course to her mother and sister. She decided she wanted to feel his cock in her mouth. (Something even more strange than a song starting in the middle of the bus.) As he watched his wife's face sink below his waistline for the first time in many years, one of the folk who sat in the middle of the bus made up his mind to insult the female members of the royal family more often in the future.

A couple of nights after Scotland vs. England, one of the folk who sat in the back of the bus was hanging about outside a chip shop wondering why he still went to football games. He liked the fighting before and after the game lots more than drinking the most or starting off the singing. He would rather have been more like Chic, one of the folk too mental to sit anywhere on the bus. He listened to Chic talking about all the folk he'd stabbed and given a good kicking. Because he'd heard Chic's stories before, he began thinking about the song that started in the middle of the bus. Before he could stop himself he began to sing,

CHARLIE'S A POOF

Chic did not join in the song, and because Chic was the nickname given to folk whose real name was Charlie, he did not like the words either. When he was recovering in hospital from being stabbed and given a good kicking, one of the folk who sat in the back of the bus decided he would be more like Chic and be one of the folk too mental to sit anywhere on the bus.

Standing among the other folk who worked in the bus station, the driver was fed up and unhappy. He did not want to attend any union meetings or to listen to speeches about cutbacks and threatened redundancies. He only liked driving and going the quickest way to the game. He began thinking about the song that started in the middle of the bus. Before he could stop himself he began to sing,

MARGARET THATCHER'S A PROSTITUTE

The other folk who worked in the bus station stopped listening to speeches about cutbacks and threatened redundancies. They all joined in the song that started in the middle of the bus. The driver no longer felt fed up or unhappy. It was as if he was comfy and stretched out on the long seat at the very back of the bus, dreaming of a time long, long ago.

Good Game, Good Game

They claim that on the 7th April
I entered the premises
occupied by Grays, Newsagent
at 1 Stenhouse Cross, Edinburgh
and stole:
a racing set
2 dolls
a model car
a beauty set
a walk bench
2 push and dance bears
a basket
11 make up sets.
The bastards forgot the cuddly toy.

ALISON FLETT

Fat Lady Sings

ahm no
a skinny wummin
trapt inside
a fat wumminz
boady

naw

ma inner selz
way way way
biggurn this

ma inner selz
FUKN HYOOJ
wi big
JUMBLIN tits
nMASSIV
swoallin nippulz
nroalls nroallsy
wobblin
tumblin
FAT
fallin
in foalds
downty ma
grate swayin buttux

ma soft
dimplin thize
ur splade
sayn
FUCK ME

ma soft
pudjy fingurz
ur splade
sayn
FUCK YOU

ahm dansin
an ma boadyz
dansin wi me
an aroond mi

whit yoo seez
jist
thi haffy it

wokkin hame

how glammurus
lit up
thi late nite bus

History of Sex in 3 Parts

1. Paradise Lost

ah wiz injoyin it that much
ah thot heed mibby
fansy a bit
so ah goze
hay adam
yoo wontin a bitty this aippul?

an bifore
ahd timety blink
thi greedy basturts
snatcht it oaff eez
an woolfd
thi fukn
loat

2. Pizzeshin

apparintly
its no mine
enny mare

its his noo
adams aippul
(hope it stix
inniz fukn throat)

3. Small Compensayshun

ah thot
rite ya basturt
think yir scrannin
aw ma fukn aippuls
then blaymin me
fur yir bellyake

well fuk yi sun

ahm oapnin ma ain
froot nvej shoap

yoo wont an aippul?
yi kin fukn pay fir it

Swimmin Wi Goggles

oan thi surfiss
faces ur thi same
no lookn it wun
anuthur

but wi goggles oan
seein underneeth
folks boadies
jentul
an sorty helpliss

wun persins moshun
beetin soft waves

up against
everywun els

all moovin
in thi same
wottur

nestling

o
thi wee burdz
i
uv yoo

blinks deep
inside
uv me

an ma hole body
melts
inty softness
surroundin
holdin
protectin

waitin ankshus
fur thi day
yoo fly

JAMES KELMAN

Some Thoughts That Morning

The subway was shaking, the subway was shaking. Yes fine, fine. And we are all vibrating; amazing eh!

But surely there is just no question about the great swathes of hypocrisy lurking in the world? It is a central part of the entire whole and takes its existence from every last single solitary thing that belongs in the world, that is part of the world.

I seem to have known for a very long time that there is a certain point and so what, what the hell does it matter: nothing is as great as all that. Nothing. No one thing can ever be said to be the driving force. Of course that is one view and there are others. No matter what one is to make of them. But what do I know? Sometimes I feel like I am not really involved in 'the world' except perhaps by association, indirect association, therefore how can certain things be said? How can anything be said? What right do I have? I do not have the right. I have no right, no rights.

Yes the subway was shaking. The other passengers vibrating and not able to do a thing about it. So what? It was one of these shifts in the tracks that could give the illusion the driver had applied the braking system on the approach to the next station. But everybody knew the truth, they had travelled these tracks for so long; every bump and turn were members of the same family. Only a stranger to this section of the subway system would make a move to get to the exit at this moment, unless in a daydream, it might be done in an absentminded condition, then realising the mistake the person would attempt some sort

135

of ridiculous cover up, trying to make out they just preferred standing or some such nonsense.

How fantastic it all is.

At the same time it is reminiscent of being in a court of law. That is what life is like. The obligation to provide evidence, to substantiate yourself. That was the way I always felt anyway. Not that I was being forced. Except sometimes I felt like that. But nobody was actually doing the forcing. But what did that matter if this was how I felt: if I felt like I was being forced then I was being forced. If one is forced one is forced. Even though pretences are played out to the bitter end.

I was fed up with it. More than anything I was fed up with these questions, fed up with my voice, the sound of my voice banging round inside my head with all these questions. These sorts of perennial conundrums to do with the whys and the wherefores; yet who cares, no one cares. Why the hell should they?

It was incredible to think everybody might be like this. An entire world full of people going about having these thoughts. Billions of heads exploding. Their faces all calm on the outside while inside this utter turmoil.

Imploding is nearer the mark. This person in front. This particular individual who sat gazing out of the window into the darkness of the tunnel, the shadows. I could not quite see his face in the window. But I had seen it when I sat down. I could barely remember it except that it was so uniquely his own. At least such is the conventional wisdom. I was viewing the populace as a series of types. I felt like twisting right round in the seat to see him. He was of the owl-class, a set distinct but not wholly dissimilar from my own. I had seen these close types before and there were minor, crucial differences. If I had been a portrait painter that would have been fine, I could have produced a big notepad and a charcoal and just said, Excuse me, and started sketching a few squiggles. I would not even have had to say 'excuse me'. Probably the guy would have accepted it quite the thing. With the advent of contemporary marketing techniques people are into the habit of having their space disrupted by strangers who were not really strangers except on an individual basis, they worked for these conglomerates and corporations whose worth everyone takes for granted; said employees have defined requirements and job-tasks necessitating the use of ordinary everyday people so ordinary everyday people put up with it; they are used to it and as a rule do not feel threatened when these company folk descend on them with a folder full of private questions about their likes and dislikes as they pertain to the use of hair shampoo or bars of chocolate.

Or else a handheld camera: Excuse me, we're here to follow you about for the next hour and a half, just pretend we're not there and carry on with your business.

The right to remain private has been withdrawn. It is now taken for granted that subject-inviolability and the market place exist conceptually but must be up for challenge at a fundamental level, that such is the mark of aforementioned inviolability in respect of the subject nowadays, through a recent legislative manoeuvre on behalf of The Majesties courtesy of This House, moved through towards the end of the last parliament, unopposed by The Loyal Opposition, that henceforth subject may be deemed object insofar as citizens are a concern.

Thoughts like this made me smile because they were so up-front politically. If I said such a thing in my place of work people would look askance. I could say these things inside my head and frequently this is what I did, most particularly in crowded situations *vis-à-vis* the public transport system.

The powers-that-be are fuckpigs.

One of those fine days such a thought could be trapped in a

137

new kind of internet, based on a form of pulse modulation. It wouldnt be too difficult.

Weighty topics.

For an instant I saw my reflection in the window. I looked good: better than fair to middling. I searched for a page of kitchen-roll I carried in my trouser pocket for emergency handkerchief purposes. It was all a pretence of course, my nose was as clean as the day is long. And the train made a singular shift in the tracks which signified we approached the next station. Sure enough the brakes were being applied, the couple of folk rising to win pole-position by the exit.

The need for a quick escape.

It was perfectly understandable. And also noticeable that parties heading the queue were both female. One might have expected the males to take the lead in their primeval role of competitive predator.

It was this being forced to find evidence all the time. Sooner or later it was guaranteed to send a body stark raving mad. And again that applied across the board. Billions of people are on the road to becoming lunatics. All because of that obligation to provide evidence. Why, in the name of all that is holy, should everybody feel so damn threatened. One looks for answers. One finds none.

People are exiting. Others are entering. One allows them their space. One sits gazing elsewhere, not forcing an undue self consciousness.

Bodies becoming uncertain of their day-to-day movements.

Being the cause of such a panic. Incredible the power of one individual, to force others into psychic turmoil; simply by looking somebody up and down, even while letting it be known that it – the look in question – is merely a look, perfomed unintentionally; wholly without malice and, on the available evidence, done in a wholly absentminded manner.

Yet still and all it would make no difference and might yet induce a panic.

These typical systems of power are so unfair. Unless one accepts that it is not a need. Yet what can be conjectured, if nothing else, is the fact that the individual person might care. But with other people sentimentality is always the risk. But why should any human being be forced to sit for whole stretches of time with their knees tightly closed as for example a woman wearing a dress. It was remotely imaginable. Not quite a nightmare so approximating to a horror story.

I had had a partner whom I did not love. Once upon a time we kept no secrets from ourselves. I had known that I did not love this partner. I questioned the notion itself and found it wanting. There was no doubt that many people loved. It had such currency it could not be doubted; if emotional facts existed in the physical world then love also existed. (Family is excluded from this equation.) But what then was I to do? In fact I knew what I had to do and that was 'nothing'. The act of doing nothing was okay, it was ample. There had been unthinkable thoughts. Certainly. Their very insubstantiality gave rise to nothing.

A woman could cross her legs. She crosses her legs and she risks further exposure. It is a risk she has to take. She is faced by such risks on a daily basis, in the company of visceral strangers, where unknowable threats are lurking. Yet what is a 'visceral' stranger?

These things occur.

The beauty of movement in the person who now sat next to me. This had been established once and for all by the entrance of other parties and their taking a seat next to her, causing her to move. The relaxed poise of that move. Perhaps she would have been more content had she been able to light a cigarette. There was no doubt she was a smoker. But what about me myself? I was a man that knew everything, right down to unknowable threats; a male at the ready, for all conceivable difficulties, e.g. some criminal-type holding up the train and waving a gun about. I would have it under control. I would have seen such reality as always possible, not imminent but possible. And I looked reasonably youthful perhaps identified as a young husband and father.

Across the aisle sat a couple in late middle-age; male and female. They had entered the carriage in conversation. They had continued this conversation. It seemed of genuine importance. It was to the exclusion of all else. Nothing the other passengers might do would ever concern them. Nor would it concern the woman seated next to me. But did it apply to myself? No, not at all, strictly speaking. These forms of self knowledge appear a wonderful thing that is the cause of great satisfaction, appearing beyond relief they result in temporary elation. I barely smiled. If I did smile it was perfunctory. Yet heightened, nervously taut.

The person next to me had become a lynchpin.

This is also strange, that I could use a word and not know what it means in its literal usage, but such a word may yet provide the most apt way of describing what it is I can feel, something that is beyond dispute, beyond the merely felt. A fact of subjective experience. I can use a metaphor to get to it, because this is what 'lynchpin' is, a metaphor for something I do not know what, not yet anyhow.

That must surely be described as positive. By this simple act of using language we take our own grip of the world. As we find it. But as of that moment I had – and always have – to stop my knee knocking against the person seated next to me, stop myself letting this other knee knock against mine. Power circuits. Static currents. Physical relationships. The modulated pulses.

Of course the outcome would prove awkward. It ever was

thus, and would remain thus. Life seems to preclude the immediate rise to the immediate occasion. Other bodies are only a further consideration. What should it matter what other people think, is a naive question. Yet it always arises. And what they did was their own affair; nothing to do with me nothing to do with them; the same as what I do is nobody's business, what a body does is not my business, and so on and so forth, round and round the rugged rock, disappearing into this circular tunnel, Hillhead east to Kelvinbridge.

I smiled, my thoughts pumping ahead. But it just was not good enough. Life: it dragged itself across one. It was not the other way about. Given His existence God did make things happen. Bodies firmly believed life was their own and they were so wrong. God's judgment was there. The unwillingness to accept reality, the God-given. It was the enormity of certain decisions appealed to me, and naturally a body should attempt to act fraudulently, to attempt the circumvention of the route, then discover a method of sustaining the blunder, even in the face of self-knowledge. Yes there was a decision and yes, it was difficult: of course it was difficult; what else could such a decision be? Even when big decisions have to be made – difficult ones (and then when one made them) – it was just a case of finding the right way to go, it was there to be found and that was what happened, one found it, but it was there all the time. That was why people didnt like you for it. They knew the decision was there to be made and they didnt want you to find it because of the pressure it put on them; because it meant they should have been finding it.

This was a moment when anyone in their right mind should have been screaming in joy or for joy. A moment when at least I should have felt like it, whether I did or not. But the pressure was off me all the same. Even getting out of this subway, knowing where I had to go, I would just sidle by people, not looking into their eyes; I would gaze at the ground, a person who just gazes at the ground; I had done it before and would do it again, I could always do it again. There are these amazing escapes and we give them to each other, despite everything.

BRENT HODGSON

Sally The Birthday Girl

This afternoon Sally Hewitt held a party to celebrate her four-teenth birthday, and during the afternoon she saw a number of ghastly sights. The party was in her own home at 20 Westwood Road and it began at 3.15. Among the gifts she received were a mini rucksack costing £10 from branches of Bhs and a bright coloured ribbed vest costing £6.99 from branches of River Island. Sally liked these two gifts very much.

The first nasty thing she saw was at a neighbour's house. A police response vehicle stopped outside of 25 Westwood Road and two officers approached Mr Bartle, the owner of a white Vauxhall Cavalier. Mr Bartle had been to the local shop and was sitting behind the wheel of his car. When questioned by the officers Mr Bartle denied robbing a nearby garage earlier that afternoon. On being hauled out of his car, Mr Bartle said he had been buying bread and milk, fruit and veg, and took out of his shopping bag a cucumber. Both officers then chose to fire their 9mm pistols at Mr Bartle, aged 38 years, who then lay on the road bleeding to death.

Sally had been enjoying herself with 15 other youngsters up to this time.

Chief Constable George Kimberly said afterwards: 'The officers of the response vehicle fired their weapons because they feared for the lives of members of the public.'

One minute later at 3.17 there was another incident. A police helicopter on aerial observation spotted a car exceeding the thirty-mile speed limit in a built-up area, and gave chase. The

motorist was travelling at 32 mph. The helicopter crashed onto
the roof of the house at 27 Westwood Road.

One woman witness said the girls at the birthday party heard
the noise of the crash and were about to run across the road to
rescue folk, when the helicopter exploded, killing the helicopter
crew and the four occupants of the house.

Chief Constable George Kimberly said afterwards: 'Any
helicopter pilot flying recklessly may reasonably make an error
of judgment.'

Sally and her friends returned to 20 Westwood Road in a
terrified state. They were comforting each other in the lounge
when they heard someone knock at the front door. Sally went
to the door. The time was 3.18.

'I am The Deathmaker,' smiled Peter Frank who was armed
with automatic weapons, his gun licence having been renewed
by British police ten days earlier. The third ghastly sight Sally
saw on her birthday, was the cold-blooded killing of her 15
friends.

Chief Constable George Kimberly said afterwards: 'Mr Frank
has been through a lot recently. His second wife moved to a new
home, taking the family pet with her, though Mr Frank had
weekend access to their dog Oscar.'

3.19 and Sally was making the mistake that adults sometimes
do when people close to them die; she was bottling up her grief.
Her mother and herself went out of the house and they were
standing at the gate when they saw a gang of thugs coming
down Westwood Road. The thugs were chanting like maniacs
and they were intent on plunder. There were householders in
the community who tried in vain to hide their valuables, but for
others the trappings of wealth suddenly did not matter. Not far
from Sally's house, a stout housewife sank dead to the ground
on seeing the thugs arrive.

The thugs, on entering houses at numbers 43, 41, 31, 26, 12

and 6 Westwood Road, wasted little time in grabbing what they could carry off. Sally and her mother locked themselves in the bathroom a moment before the thugs came in. On returning to the lounge when the house was silent, Sally could not find her ribbed vest or her mini rucksack, and her pair of 50s-style shades had also been stolen.

Chief Constable George Kimberly said afterwards: 'We urge members of the public whose homes have been broken into, to apprehend and beat to death those responsible. Housebreakers can be found in taverns, there being no shortage of thieves in such places. Rich men like solicitors and politicians whose houses have been emptied, might like to avoid the persecution and murder of men of lesser calibre than themselves, by diverting their minds to fine music.

'I can recommend the sound recordings of chamber music held by the East German Radio's central library, who deserve great credit for preserving their country's musical heritage, especially the sinfonies of Johann Philipp Kirnberger.'

Sally experienced a fifth ghastly sight at 3.20. Through the window facing the road Sally saw the appearance of a group of public relations experts wearing masks, who marched down the road demanding the abolition of lecture halls set aside for the teaching of journalists. To show they meant business they petrol-bombed several houses – numbers 34, 26, 18 and 8 Westwood Road, and when this was done, they fired their machine guns at human targets. The family of Mr Alf Brown who lived next door to Sally, were unlucky in respect of their lives; on escaping from their burning house all five members of the family met a hail of bullets. Sally gave a cry when she saw Alf, in his wheel chair, slump forward.

Chief Constable George Kimberly said afterwards: 'I think the PR people have a point. Why should we read publications

written by journalists? I am sick of reading their bland inter-
views, monotone news stories, and their coverage of cultural
events is patchy.

'There is a gap in the market for news on social affairs and, in
my opinion, PR people and pressure groups should be allowed
to provide material to fill that gap.'

At 3.31 Sally heard the shout: 'Stay where you are! We are
doing house calls!'

Two lorries had pulled up in front of her house. The low,
flat decks of the lorries were piled with corpses. Men who were
following the lorries picked up Mr Bartle and flung him on,
even though he was not quite dead. The men, twenty or so of
them, were a stinking, sweaty gang.

Sally and her mother went to the lounge window. The men
were entering houses in which there were no flames. Instant
rape was the order of the day for any woman found alive.
Death for untended babies was just as rapid. Mrs Hewitt, who
was normally a strong woman, had little strength left when she
cuddled her daughter and said, 'What a day your birthday is
turning out to be. You hear about things like this all the time
on TV, but when it is happening on your own doorstep, it is
a real shock.'

A man of overpowering stench walked through the door of
number 20 Westwood Road. Mrs Hewitt pushed her daughter
to the floor and told her not to move a muscle. Sally was on the
floor clutching the dead shoulder of her friend Mandy Brown,
when the eyes of her mother greeted the man who came into
the room.

Chief Constable George Kimberley said afterwards: 'On
learning of an outbreak of civil disorder this afternoon, I sent
a couple of meat wagons to Westwood Road to pick up the
dead and dying.

'I would like to thank the governor of the city jail for the

release of 22 prisoners, all of whom assisted in the cleaning-up
operation. Thanks Archie, see you at the club tonight.'

Today I Visited Marilyn

Marilyn is a woman who once had a lovely head of brunette
    hair,
and who lives in a flat with just the one bedroom.
As we near the end of the 20th century,
I am glad that Marilyn does not choose to be out to visitors.
I was reminded today that winter is here again;
rain, wind and cold, and some people say that winter
in a rural village of 16th-century France was an eventless
    time,
but these people must have been thinking of life all
    year round
in modern-day Britain.
Marilyn and I live on a housing estate
and our lives are not spent bringing in hay or driving wolves
    from flocks
or grafting young fruit trees in the tree nursery;
nor do we travel the country equipped with cloth and tape
    and scissors
to measure our neighbours for suits of new clothes.
We have only an approximate idea of time.
Things happen when they happen.
Marilyn has a clock upstairs but she never looks at it.
Like my own life, her life is private and internalised,

though I have heard rumours she had an affair and possibly a
   child
with a computer programmer who lived further down
   the street.
I visit Marilyn in her kitchen, the warmest room in her flat.
She sleeps there, and on occasion she wakes up to find me
standing patiently by her bedside.
She gets dressed in front of me and then without any great
   ceremony,
we have hot drinks and a bite to eat.
Outside of our world a circle of people plod on,
returning to their homes when no hands are needed
for a few hours work in a shop, office or factory.
A small-scale sense of wholeness still prevails in the urban
   civilisation:
one day, in the summer of 1995, while Marilyn was sitting in
   the kitchen,
she bought a couple of packets of tablets off a wee girl
who had knocked at her door.
In these times of despair I shudder and count my blessings:
Marilyn is a friend of mine.
Today I visited Marilyn.
She was wearing her oiled overall and hat,
her false nose filled with purifying spices;
a nose that was large and in imitation of a bird's beak.
'Give me a rush, something quick and cheap,' I said,
and using her wand, she felt for my pulse.

Floral Videos

For sale: Uncensored Videos.

Available NOW by mail order from Floral Videos of
  Amsterdam.

Please do NOT write to us for details.

Due to the non-stop action of these adult videos,

explicit details will be supplied only after you have placed
  your order.

Each 3-hour video costs £55. Send a cheque or remittance
  to:

Floral Videos, PO BOX 700, Amsterdam.

Choose one, two or three videos from our list:

3 hours of Yellow Daffodils – being lashed in a shower
  of rain;

3 hours of White Daffodils – standing proud and erect;

3 hours of Golden Daffodils – in full bloom, revealing all.

THREE INCREDIBLE VIDEOS WITH DIALOGUE IN
  INTERNATIONAL ENGLISH.

Warning: these videos may cause offence if viewed by your
  Granny.

Floral Videos can make up a VERY SPECIAL order just
  for you.

This way you can be sure of viewing exactly what appeals
  to you.

Simply tell us what you would like to see, and our experts
  will make a film to meet your personal tastes.

Spend over £110 with Floral Videos and you will receive

completely FREE a bumper pack of high-quality goods: a hand spade 10″ in length; an inflatable knee cushion; the latest edition of the *Weeders Digest*.

And Customers! Please remember that Floral Videos are NOT advertised in so-called HARD-CORE GARDENING MAGAZINES.

ROBERT ALAN JAMIESON

Antikksiemen

These sea poems are extracted from the first section of *Blown Worldwise: an intertextual voyage*, which combines lyric with a fictional treatment of the Cutty Sark's epic twelfth voyage, and short essays on 'Burns, Jamaica and Post-Imperialist Conscience'. This complex of writings forms a kind of autobiography, but one that reaches outward from the personal/local to the national and supranational. The first section of *Blown Worldwise* includes notes on the genesis and orthography of the poems. An edited version of these notes follows below.

The realisation of my first tongue – 'Shetlin', or Shetlandic, as it was spoken in the 1960s on the westmost point of the main island – in a written form continued to intrigue and frustrate me for a long time, till finally I began to create dual-language text. Released from the dilemma of attempting to find an equilibrium between reader-access and idiolect, the problem then was to create a consistent orthographic system which would allow readers inclined to attempt pronunciation to do so. This search for phonetic accuracy led me gradually to the realisation that the English alphabet was inadequate for my purpose.

Besides the peculiar word-stock and grammatical forms, the main distinctive feature of the 'Shetlin' I learned as a boy was the presence of 'Scandinavian' vowels. To render these, I began to make use of the symbols ø (diphthong, from low throat 'u' as in English 'up' progressing quickly to high front 'e' as in

151

English 'see'); **ö** (similar in quality to the French 'peu'); and **æ**, the 'Anglo-Saxon *ash*' which was replaced by 'e' or 'ee' in the 13th century and lost from the English alphabet, before being reintroduced for the representation of the Latin 'æ' during the Renaissance – **æ** has a strong claim to be included in representation of all Scots dialects, as one of the hallmarks of Scots difference from English is that it did not undergo the sound changes which led to the loss of the graph 'æ' in Southern Standard English. The doubling **aa** represents a characteristic long vowel of Shetlandic, pronounced as in the English exclamation 'Aah!' The phonetic value '*i*', as in 'Psych*i*', is generally represented by the combination **ie**, although in some instances the English or Scots form has been preserved purely for clarity of meaning, as with the digraphs 'sea/see' or 'wie/we'.

The process led to the adoption of other non-standard English conventions: the use of the symbol **j** where English uses **y** corresponds to other Germanic languages and is useful because it frees the symbol **y** for sole use as representative of the sound given phonetically as '*i*', as in the English 'eye'. The effect of this is that symbol **i** can exclusively represent the phonetic value i, as in English 'sit'.

To avoid confusion, the graph combinations **gh** and **ch** represent, respectively, the velar fricative 'x' as in Scots 'loch' or Irish 'lough', and the English affricate 'tʒ' as in 'ditch'. The latter is also used for 'dʒ', as in the English 'judge' as the distinction locally between the two is slight. The **quh** form represents 'kw', as in older Scots forms like those of William Dunbar, which is still spoken in parts of Shetland, where it corresponds to the English 'qu', as in 'quick', but also 'wh', as in 'why' or 'where'. Additionally, where in modern Scots and English reversals (metathesis) has taken place, 'Shetlin' or Shetlandic retained the original form at least up until the 1960s, hence 'gi**r**ss' rather than 'grass'.

The product is an outlandish looking language, I admit, but that is consistent with my first tongue, formed in the village of Sannis in the west of Shetland in the late 50s and 60s – geographically, an outlandish situation. In this sense, it is not related to the 'Synthetic Scots' of MacDiarmid – because it is rooted in a time-specific spoken form. It is local language poetry, but it emerges out of a singular relation with that locality.

Thematically, in the sequence which these lyrics are part of, I have sketched an ongoing 'figure of outward,' as Charles Olson terms it, which could be expressed in the local as 'frammir': the direction away from home port. These short narrative poems begin from an autobiographical source, but are intended to reach beyond the experience of the child I was, to become an elegy for a way of life now largely lost – the Merchant Navy, 'da sælin'. For this reason and because there are now thirty years between my present situation and the self at the heart of these poems, they are written in the third person.

Glossary:

toom – thumb; **piltiks** – coalfish; **sprikkil** – wriggle; **glæp** – gulp; **firnenst** – behind, below; **noost** – a shelter for a boat, dug into the beachhead; **njoosin** – gossip; **hømin** – summer twilight; **twaartrie** – a few (lit. 'two or three'); **bunghsie** – arctic skua; **neb** – beak; **biggin** – building; **kjittil** – tickle; **ettil** – sense, realise; **niesik** – porpoise; **guddik** – riddle; **krægs** – rocks; **bød** – pub, (lit. 'booth'); **jeg kjenner mine folk** – a Norwegian saying, meaning 'I'm among my own people'; **oob** – howl; **gjing** – go; **boosin** – buffeting; **wrakk** – destruction; **aan** – own; **spølie** – scatter; **abøn** – above

At Da Eela

Æ fyn nyght
lyn fyshin
wie sum oda aald men –

lissnin t'stoaries
as sjærp as da sie ær –

a hjook slips his grip,
kuts trow wiet skjin,
tærs his toom opin,
an he fiels da saat byt.

Haalt fæ da depts,
piltiks sprikkil, glissnin,
glæpin fir waatir,
gills flaapin, die.

Blød fæ da hjook mark
drips
ida osjin –

glæmin broon sea lævs o tang
swiem firnenst da grien spaars
in a kaald wiet wirld

as da lyns wind oot.

AT THE EELA: the inshore summer fishing, which supplied many a winter meal with dried, salted fish. Originally the term referred to the habit of anchoring the boat at tried and tested places, from *Old Norse 'ili', a stone with a rope fastened to a boat and serving as an anchor.*

Botabit

Wun asjoair, da boat up
ida noost, da tekkil sortit,
hit's mæsjirt in bukkits,
dievydit atwien hoosis.

Da pyps ir oot,
da riek kloods roond,
da njoosin lingirs,
ida hømin.

'Ja,'
he'll tak twaartrie dær
tæ Miena's porch-doar.

'Heir,'
prood o da pukkil
gien t'dem dat hedna mukkil.

She taks da pælfoo fæ him,
an she bids him 'Kum de wis,'
an she maks him sit
an staps him bannik-foo.

BOTABIT: the division of the catch between those who had shared in
the fishing, often including a portion to the elderly or sickly of the village,
from *Old Norse*, *'bata-byti', the sharing out from a boat.*

Koors Saat an Snaa

Twa dæs eftir,
he waaks amung da
waashin lyns o dryin fysh
hingin ootsyd hoosis –

læk kut-oot strings
o chojint-up men
da bærns mak
wie fowldit pæpir
an a pær o sjiers.

Siks munt lætir,
ida hert oda wintir,
wie da snaa apo da ært,
da unjin in da pikkil drum
willa mæd da maachik happin –

an a saat tung wil mynd apo
dat lang simmir nyght
quhan da katsh wis tæn.

COARSE SALT AND SNOW: Cleaned and gutted fish were hung
to dry outside and then, later, inside near the peat fire. The means
of discovering when the pickling salt-and-water mixture was the right
consistency involved placing an onion in the barrel, to see whether
it floated.

Tæ Da Hum

In a tin boie's imachinæsjin,
fattint up wie R.L.S,
jun pyrit tæls rin færlie wyld –

quhar da died bunghsie hings
bie a klaa, upsyd doon
on da hyght o da hill,

da bløted fæ da sjot in hit's briest
a waarnin
t'da hoarnie nebs
dat speir a njoo-boarn lam.

Quharin an aald biggin,
mæbie fæ dæis
quhan Yriesh munks
upræst stæns in ootby plæsis,
he fiels an ingklin
o a bersærk's kjittil
an ettils at da livin storie
o træsjir fun in fiftie-æght
apo Sint Ninjin's Ajl
mann ryght enjoch bie troo.

Twintie-æght piesis o silvir
an da chaabon o a niesik –
a Piktiesh troav wie a guddik kroon.

TO THE UNINHABITED HOLM: the Holm of Melby lies only a few hundred metres offshore from Melby beach. St Ninian's Isle in the south of Shetland is similarly close to the township of Bigton, connected by a sand bar, or tombola. Here in 1958, a schoolboy assisting on an archaeological dig uncovered a valuable treasure at the old Celtic church. The purpose of the porpoise is uncertain. The tales of dolphins and porpoises guiding ships may have something to do with it.

Da Dæj Chim Haakins Enchin Kut Oot

Ida middla Papa Soond an
fædir saa him, staandin aft,
wævin his jaalloo ojilskjin brieks –

foand da kostgærd,
panikt, a sens o horrir
as he siemt t'drift
apo da Hum o Melbie
ida ræs o tyd –

ræl fær aroond –

dan rielief
as da boat
kliert da krægs

an hædit ootby
t'da opin waatirs
o Sint Magnis Bæ,
quhar da lyfboat
pikkit him up.

Bettir ös a man
nivir mæd o his brieks,
Bobbie sæd.

THE DAY JIM HAWKINS ENGINE CUT OUT: the family name of
Hawkins, with its *Treasure Island* connotation, was brought to Sandness
by the much-loved Church of Scotland missionary, Rev. Cecil Hawkins,
some of whose family subsequently settled there.

158

Lament Fir Da Tristie

Kösjin Dan wis lost,
hædit fir Hillswiek
akross Sint Magnis Bæ
on a koors nyght
in an opin boat.

Fok sæd
he wis gjaain
til da bød dær
fir drink.

He tinks – Aa dat waatir!
          Man, hit's dry
          t'die o drooth
          amung sæ mukkil waatir.

LAMENT FOR THE THIRSTY: The westside of Shetland was 'dry'
through most of the current century, having been particularly influenced
by the Temperance movement. Not that this prevented people from
drinking. But it did mean that those who wanted a bottle would have to
arrange circuitous methods to obtain it, or undertake what was sometimes
a hazardous journey.

Vestenfra

Kaptin Goardin
gied t'sæl
da Norrowa kost,
kærjin kærgo
nort an sooth,
in an oot trow
fjord an fjell.

Færd at first
t'opin his mooth,
till he began t'hier
a lok o wirds
he toght he kent
fæ hæm wir bein
spokkin heir aboot.

'Sjetlandsk,' he sæs,
dightin himsel.
'Sjetlandsøyene.'
An dæ nod dir hedds,
da Norskies,
an wi a kynda Sjetlin
soond, sae 'Ja.'

He tinks – Jeg kjenner mine folk –
wir æn fokk.

FROM THE WEST (Norwegian): The axis north to south, to Scotland, has been the Shetlander's main route for centuries, mirroring the political shift away from Scandinavia. The journey eastward to Norway, though historically important, had been much less travelled in recent times, until the establishment of new sea and air networks in the post-oil North Sea. But there were always the sailors, whose work carried them to these shores from the west, who recognised there the familiar language of home.

Hy Syd Agæn, Bojis!

Bobbie o da aald Haa,
his mukkil oobin laagh
boosin lugs, tells agæn
his best-kent tæl –

aboot da kroo o laandlubbirs
wir sælin trow a hevie swall
an quhan dir boat began
t'pitch an rowl, wid run
fæ port t'starboard, fæ
starboard back t'port
t'try an kiep a levil dekk.

Da showt gied up –
'Hy syd agæn, bojis!
Hy syd agæn!'

He tinks – Ja, choost læk wis fok,
    t'gjing skuttirin ers first,
    tinkin at we'r døin ryght,
    quhile we mak wirsels siek.
    An quhan we ken we'r wirkit
    folie, we wiss t'Gød we hedna,
    bit winna aan da wrakk we'r med,
    bekaas we klem we kent næ bettir.

HIGH SIDE AGAIN, BOYS!: The story-teller referred to here was also named Robert Jamieson but was no relation to the present writer. The change from the patronymic naming system in the eighteenth century meant that anyone whose father's name was James became a Jamieson, making genealogy, known locally as 'reddin kin', a fascinating study full of false leads.

Bobby was a merchant seaman in his youth and had brought a wife home from Middlesbrough. They lived in the Aald Haa – the old laird's hall – at the head of Melby pier, next to the more imposing 'Mukkil Haa', where the last of the Sandness lairds, the Scotts of Melby, had lived up until they lost their estate around the turn of the last century.

Dø Wiel An Persieveir

Ahint da aald skøl waa,
tryjin smokkin fags,
da mestir's step
aroond da koarnir
sends dim spøliejin awaa,
riek kummin oota
mooths, poochis, girss.

Abøn dir heds, abøn da doar,
da motoo set dær i dir hærts
kærvt ida stæn –
'Dø wiel an persieveir'.
Da wirds o Ertie Aandirsin,
exampil t'wis aa, dæ sæ,
him at gied an læd da foond
o an empyr's pryd an choie –
da P&O lyn boie.

He tinks – Na boie, empyrs næ mær.
          Da merchint nævie's fieniesht.
          Gjing du, du'll fin næ empyr dær.

DO WELL AND PERSEVERE: the school motto of the Anderson Educational Institute, founded by Arthur Anderson, who had started his working life as a beach boy. When he left Shetland to join the Navy in 1808, these were the parting words of his employer. Anderson went on to become co-founder of the Peninsular & Oriental shipping line. He was a great benefactor in Shetland in the later nineteenth century, and in 1847 became the first Member of Parliament for Orkney and Shetland not drawn from the privileged, landed families.

162

DUNCAN McLEAN

The Shearing

She left him hunched at the end of the bed, the green light of the telly shining on his brow and his cheekbones, and the taut muscles of his neck.

The Arms was empty cause of the lambing. She sat on the middle stool, then got down and moved to the left-hand one, where she could rest her back on the wall under the display case of dusty cigars. She stared straight ahead and waited for Stewart to finish his phone call.

I ken it was for charity, Stewart was saying. I ken it's a good cause. But it makes no odds: if you're having a race night, you have to have races, not slow bloody motion. Did Red Rum *stroll* around Aintree?

He listened for half a minute, holding the phone away from his face to mouth, Hi Yvonne, and roll his eyes.

Listen, he said, clamping the thing back to his lug. All I'm saying is, next time, send a projector that runs at the right bloody speed. Folk were laying bets and having to wait twenty minutes for the race to end! They're under starters orders . . . they're off . . . and . . . okay folks, talk amongst yourselves for half an hour, I'll wake you for the last furlong.

Yvonne felt in her pockets, drew out the cash, and dumped it on the bar. Notes she smoothed and pushed off to one side. Coins she separated into brown and silver, and lined up in rows. Then, one at a time, she picked up the coppers and fed them into the slot in the neck of the big whisky bottle on the bar. The label showed a photo of a smiling man and a dog on a lead, both wearing dark glasses.

When she came to the end of the coppers, she hesitated, then leant forward, frowning, and examined the label. The man really was blind, but somebody'd just drawn the shades on the dog for a laugh. Really it could see fine.

Aye well, said Stewart. Aye well. Well. If there *is* a next time. I wouldn't bet on it.

And he dropped the receiver into its cradle.

Bloody chancer, he said, and stepped over to lean on the bar along from Yvonne. Had to have a lock in. Folk here till half-two and we still only made seventy quid. Pathetic! How much of a kidney machine's that going to buy, do you think? A new set of tyres for the trolley maybe!

Stewart, she said. Get us a bloody drink.

Eh? Oh, aye.

Dark rum, she said, and started feeding her row of silver into the big bottle.

Stewart lowered the glass from the gantry, nudged the optic till the last couple drops plopped into the tumbler. Anything in it? he said.

Aye, more rum.

A double? Sure, sure. He turned back to the gantry. That'll be . . . two sixty.

The smallest I've got's tenners, she said, then frowned at the blind folks' bottle again. Jesus – I just put sixty in there! More!

Stewart laid down her drink, scratched the back of his head. I don't think I can break it open if you're wanting it back, he said. We need a celebrity to do that. Last time we got that golfer off the telly, mind. Smashed the thing with a seven iron.

I ken, said Yvonne. I was there. We were picking glass out of our peanuts for hours.

Stewart laughed. Still, all for a good cause, eh.

Put another rum in there, she said, nodding at the untouched tumbler on the wee towel in front of her.

Stewart picked up the glass, paused. Another double? he said.

Yvonne blinked. No, you growk. Just the one.

He scooshed in more drink, carried it carefully across to her, and held out his hand for the three ninety.

She used her pinkie to steer the tenner across the vinyl towards him. He snatched it up, chunked open the till, and slapped a fiver, a pound coin and a ten pence piece on the bar.

Yvonne immediately posted the ten into the blind-bottle slot, then gazed at the five and the one. Do you not have a pound note? she said. I don't like yon coins.

Stewart opened the till, peered in, shook his head.

Yvonne sighed.

I could give you two fifties.

No, she said.

Five twenties.

I don't want any coins, she said. I don't like them. She picked up the pound and slotted it away. It slithered down the scree of smash in the bottle and clinked against the glass. The trouble with coins, she said, They go flying out of your pooches if you drop your jeans ower fast.

Ho ho! cried Stewart, slapping his hand down on the bar.

Yvonne lifted the rum, swallowed half in a oner. Don't laugh, she said. Unless it's funny. Is it? Eh?

What? said Stewart. Pardon?

Does it make you laugh, the idea of having sex with me?

The idea of . . . with you? Yvonne! God's sake! His eyes flicked around the empty bar. Nicol . . .   he whispered.

Nicol's not here, she whispered back. He's at home with his blessed livestock.

Lambing?

Aye lambing. Morning, noon and night.

Stewart hunched his eyebrows. Out all night, eh?

Worse than that. He rigged up a video link from the shed to the bedroom, so if he woke in the night he'd see whether any of them'd dropped. But Christ, he sits up till the wee hours now, watching the bloody box. He eats his dinner in front of it. He can't take his eyes off it. Doesn't even see me!

Stewart glanced towards the door. He's up there now is he?

Aye.

Watching the yowes?

Aye.

He cleared his throat. Catherine's at her mother's.

So? Yvonne narrowed her eyes.

Well, what you were saying about having sex . . . great! Come on ben. The place is dead thenight anyway. Let's go for it.

Stewart . . .

I've always wanted to, he said, moving along till he was right across the counter from her. Well, I don't mean . . . it's not like every time you come in with Nicol I'm *looking* at you, *thinking* about it. But now you bring it up, now I do start to think about it, to think about what I think, well: you're one sexy lady, Yvonne, no doubt about it.

He looked down at his reflection in the polished bar top for a second, shook his head.

I don't ken what it is with me and Catherine, he went on. But we've lost the spark, ken? I mean, by the time I've finished here, I'm fit for nothing. But not tonight. Tonight feels different. I'm sparking tonight!

He started loosening his tie, flicked his head towards the backshop and the stairs up to the flat. Come on, he said. I'll close up early. Come on.

Yvonne picked up her glass, looked at Stewart over the

edge of the rum, then drained it. She jumped down from the stool.

Stewart, she said. I didn't ask if you wanted to shag me. I just asked if the idea of it made you laugh.

He was fiddling to undo the top button on his shirt now. It doesn't, he said. It makes me . . .

I ken, I ken, she said, holding up her hands. You don't have to tell me. She backed away from the bar, towards the door. I appreciate your reaction, Stew, she said. I really do. But don't get too het up back there. Cause I'm off home. She'd reached the door.

Oh bugger, said Stewart, tie hanging skew-whiff. I've been daft, have I?

Forget it, she said. Honestly.

He bent forward from the waist to rest his forehead on the bar-top.

Buggeration . . .

Sorry, Stewart, she said, and walked out.

Yvonne hurried through the village, head down. She turned off through the trees opposite the school, then off again up the track to the Mains. As she strode up the long slope, she watched the windows. All were dark, except for upstairs right, the bedroom. Faint green light flickered there: he hadn't even bothered to close the curtains.

She walked on, passed the porch, crossed the court, and stopped at the door to the sheep-shed. She hesitated for a moment, then moved quickly, unzipping her jacket and dropping it to the ground, pulling her jumper and shirt over her head, toeing off her boots, rugging down her jeans. No coins went spilling across the concrete. Shivering now, she took off her pants, socks and bra. Her nipples were poking with the cold. So much the better.

She slid open the shed door, and stepped forwards into the

dimly lit space with its smell of malty-feed, hay and dung. She walked into the aisle between the pens, heard the animals shift and stir on their straw, watching.

Was he watching too? She turned towards the end of the shed, threw her arms out wide, and lifted her head to look up at the camera hanging from the rafter there. A little red eye blinked back at her.

She waited.

JANICE GALLOWAY

this much is constant

Home is where you make it.
Childhood is never outgrown; only, with determination,
adapted, reviewed, refined. Fear and wonder are constants.

Childhood is where you make it.
Determination is never outgrown; only with fear and wonder
adapted, reviewed, refined. Home is a constant.

Wonder is where you make it.
Home is never outgrown, only, with Childhood Fear, reviewed,
refined, adapted Determination is a

you is where Fear is never outgrown you

Wonder you review you make it refined with

Childhood is constant you never make it

Home is
Home is

Home is where

bones grating against each other

black holes black　ho

　　　　　　　　　　ho

　　　　　　　　　　o

　　　　　　　　　　　o

　　　　　　　　　this is

　　　　　　　　　this is

　　　　　　　　　there is

　　　　　　　　　make up.

　　　　　　　　　Mother's red lipstick on a crocheted mat.

　　　　　　　　　This is my home.
　　　　　　　　　Say it is bright the bright one say

　　　　　　　　　　　　　　　　　　　it

　　　　　　　　　　　　　　　　　　　is

　　　　　　　　　　　　　　　　　　　a

　　bright room with beige flowers. Tan leaves and orange
stripes. The same wallpaper on every wall. The curtains are
so white and you can see right through them when it's sunny.
Fibreglass. Fibre made of glass. When you touch, they shock
your fingers. Sometimes if you look hard, really hard, you see
the sparks. You try not to touch them because of the shocks and
because of the whiteness. You need to be careful or you leave
marks. Tell-tale marks. Breath on the window makes a bloom
like dragon-breath on the clean pane. Your breath. Past those
twin circles is outside with the washing line, scrubby grass; tattie
shaws in irregular clumps on a patch of grey earth. Rhubarb
and potatoes. Things you can eat. Sometimes there is a dog

or a cat pushing at something near the bins. There is only dirt inbetween the visible leaves. At the front, though, there are rosebushes. Roses, dahlias, night-scented stock. Out on the porch in the dark, holding the snib back till your thumb knuckle goes white so it doesn't make a noise, you have seen the moon coming out behind cloud, inhaled the smell of them mixed with rain.

The washing throws shadows. Shifting shapes.

In front of the naked potato drills, jumpers wave their arms.

They would be stiff if it was winter, sprouting frost like hairs. They would hurt your fingers. Shadows reach for the window when they see you watching, change their minds. Clouds nose about the sky like strays. Shadows. Clouds.

Maybe it's not as light as you thought.

Maybe it's almost dark.

Dim grainy air so the posters you have tacked on the wall are just blots. You know who they are though, know what they must be from habit. Doris Day and the Beatles, The Man from UNCLE with his lips painted over in nailpolish so you can kiss him and he won't spoil. Elvis in some kind of American soldier uniform is so far into the shade you can only see sheen. The wardrobe and dressing table look black. On top of the dresser, the ancient cylinder of talc, a brush and comb set, bits of make-up glimmer as though through murky water. Mother's make-up. Scarlet. It makes your lips scar

on a crocheted mat the mat is beige with a pink trim. The mirror.

Take your time. The mirror.

The mirror is full of orange bedspread. It has cigarette holes in, a frilly trim that trails down to the carpet but you can't see the carpet. Orange quilted pillow slips. You can't see any of these things. Turn round though. You turn around and there they are, the colours less acid, tangible. Beside the bed, the cabinet with mother's books inside, their spines angled so you can't read them unless you move them on purpose. You have moved them on purpose plenty of times. *Angelique, The Practical Home Doctor* and *TRUE CRIMES* magazine underneath. *TRUE CRIMES* has creases on the cover and a scared woman running. You have no idea what she is running away from but it will be something. You have no doubt it's the right thing she's doing. You slide them back as exactly as you can manage, replace the wing-topped specs. Even after all this practice, it makes you uneasy, putting them back and hoping you haven't left smears on the lenses, a fingerprint. On the other side of the bed, *Alice Through the Looking Glass* with plasticine stains on the picture of Humpty Dumpty. His swollen belly or neck or whatever it is is all torn off; it is eroded and smells funny. It smells of being small, wearing plastic sandals and lint. Green. The plasticine was green. There are jotters here too, little ink footprints on the corners, marching off the edge. They have nowhere to run. Whose jotters are these? These are JANE's jotters. Her pencils have chew marks down to the lead. Black graphite tips between her teeth. A sheet with the beginnings of a story lies on the floor. It hangs on one snapped sentence, waiting. A drawing of a tree with no leaves.

TV. There's TV on. A man's voice.

It comes through the ceiling. THE ITHER CHANNEL SADIE SWITCH ON THE OTHER YIN and a comedy show comes on, laughing. They are up there walking about over your head. These are your neighbours. They have white hair. The light fittings flutter when they move. You've been in this room a long time and the tv never gets any quieter. Muttering, laughter,

muttering, applause and catcalls. Cat. Calls. They start too. You never get the jokes. Look at the ca
rpet. No-
body
is down
there.

There is nobody down there.

You can jump on the floor all night and disturb nothing. No one will tell you to stop. Unless. Unless they look in. In the corner of the room next to the single sheets of piano score, your sensible straps, a hairnet bunched in on itself like a dead spider and n

othing in the far corner of the room, a
brass fruit bowl with n

othing

But you can't keep from looking at it forever.

You can't pretend it's not there.

A fire vent over the bedhead, its handle, waiting to open or shut the grille. It glints like teeth in the dark, makes a sound like sore bones. You don't want to get any closer but it is coming anyway, sidling up. Without wanting to, you lift your eyes to the s-shaped slits. Draw your eye to the beautiful moulded rims. Look. Careful of dust, blown-back soot, the smell of burning, look. It is

thick orange and green brocade

a sound
less

this is my home my
home the

place where I live with my mummy lives my
mummy and my big sister and my

h

o

me is a

room with no door.

Just a curtain at the top of a stairwell over a close. The
single window overlooks a brown street, shops. A barber's with
a blood-striped lance juts from the opposite wall, a plain brown
window with the name VIRGINIA in gold on a navy ground.
A woman's name. VIRGINIA. Over the roofs, gulls. The sky
is gunboat grey even at this time in the afternoon. Salt deposits
on the glass. Marks like dried spit. This is your home.
Home your house this is where you live.
Turn.

A red divan so close to the window recess it needs pushed aside
to get past. It goes wall to wall, back to the light. There are spots
through the redness if you concentrate, different colours: yellow
ochre, olive green, steel blue, albino-flesh white, circled with a
thin line of grainy black. Like fish eyes. Move around the divan
frame and they do too, following. There are two sides to this
room. This is one. It is full of the divan. If it was opened it would
fill almost the whole place but it is never opened till night and

even then there is still enough room to watch tv. The tv. It's
on the other side, perching on a side-table, still close enough to
touch. It might even be on. Test Card: black and white squares
and a medley of Scottish Military Airs. Pipes and drums. You've
watched it before, waiting for something to come on. Sometimes
something does. Next to it is the fireplace, swirly tiles and a
green rug with two burn holes where live coals have fallen. The
holes have a weal round the outside, like a crater, something off
a picture of the moon or where pus has oozed out of your face
only the edges are hard. They scratch. Fire burns round holes.
Perfect ellipses. Over the fire – it is not on, the grate is swept
– there is the bakelite radio, the copper-colour alarm clock, the
brass of Queen Elizabeth I in a down-to-the-floor dress and
a ruff round her neck her eyes blank like a vampire and two
porcelain people in Arcadian costumes. They are all on the
mantelpiece. The porcelain maybe it is china. It breaks. It isn't
broken but it breaks keep away don't touch. It is a man and
a woman turned away from each other she has a half-opened
fan and half-smile and he has knee-breeches and a tricorn hat,
hands out-turned like an Indian dancer. Cocky. White faces and
rosebud mouths

like
like

remember the time you found the mouse under the sink in a trap
its nose turned up like it just smelled something nice to eat only
its spine got snapped instead nobody told you not to look under
there maybe they thought it was ok you would never find it so
you didn't tell just you got sick but nothing came up thinking
about its whiskers sticking up that way as though it was looking
for something good and this trap with the spring, loaded and
waiting for it in the dark when it was distracted by a promise.

Snap. Snap. It was lucky you didn't get a row they didn't find out. Maybe it's in there now. Behind the wee cream-coloured doors under the sink.

Through the gap in the wall, look and see.

The cream-coloured door, the red vegetable rack and Baby Belling a two-ring Baby Belling it's called Baby pretending to be a kitchenette. A pink potty is under there somewhere, the inside all scoured from scrubbing, squint on a pile of newspaper. That's what you were looking for when you found the mouse. The mouse was on a piece of wood it was looking up at the top of the wee cupboard, looking for something, its eyes tiny round balls. And it didn't move. It didn't move because there was a spike in the wood a skewer in the wood a barb jagging up through its tiny neck and don't look now. Don't. For now, it doesn't matter.

The ceiling.

I don't know what colour the ceiling is.

Maybe I never looked at it. Maybe I listened.

Mother is under the floorboards. That noise is her, moving about cleaning something. It could be anything. She is not angry. You can tell from the cleaning sounds. They are not too loud. Worn-smooth bouclé cloth of the divan beneath bare legs, people's feet passing on the paving outside, the odd car engine, weans shouting. The half-light on the manilla coloured wallpaper and Dettol off the stairs become one. Iodine, ancient fur coat, the acrid stink of dross and matches waiting in the grate. Before it is completely dark, mother's slipper soles will begin dragging like corpses on the stone steps, coming cl

o

o

there is

make-up
mother's red lipstick on a crocheted mat
you can't keep from looking forever

Through the s-shaped slits, her eyes.
Her pupils are black holes.

Watching back.

ALI SMITH

Instructions for Pictures of Heaven

Faces

The woman in the fruit shop has a face like bruised fruit.

If you sit on the benches people think you're unemployed. That makes some people ignore you and some people stop to sit beside you. Some of them are mad, the ones who pass as well as the ones who stop and sit down. You can pretty much tell by their faces. Your instinct is getting good now for telling which is which. When they walk past and ignore you it is easier to look properly at their faces. Whereas, if someone is sitting beside you talking to you and you look him or her (usually him) in the face then he thinks you're looking at him for some reason like you want something or you fancy him or you want to give him something or tell him something. You have to be careful.

It doesn't even matter if you only sit on the bench for a minute. People who see you there still think what they like about you. It's the same if you stand about outside anywhere in the middle of town, say if you're waiting for someone, or especially if you squat down on the pavement or sit on a step because you're tired. Then people look away because they think you're going to ask them for money. Some even give you some even though you're not asking for money. You'd be rubbish on the street. You wouldn't know what to do.

It's busy. It must be lunch hour. They've started selling barbecued chicken in the Co-op Local. The Co-op Local is its new name; last year it was called the Stop'N Shop, and before that it was called the 8 til' Late. Before that it was called something else, you can't remember. Anyway you are quite pleased with yourself for remembering as much as you do about the names of it. A lot of people go past here all the time, and probably none of them remembers about the other names, or even notices about them changing like you notice.

You stretch your toes inside your shoe. Your shoes are new, to you, and not quite the right size; you need a heelgrip or something. A child goes past and it has a face like a frog. A woman goes past and her face is like a plank of wood. A younger woman goes past; she has a face like she is supposed to have, all in the right place, that is what young women are supposed to look like, like someone out of Kays' Catalogue except in a bad temper. An old man goes past. He goes past most days when you're here. His face is lined and grey like the trunk of a tree. He smiles at you and more lines break all over his face. He goes so slowly past you that it is like his smile is in slow motion.

You can watch the faces, there are always more of them. Or you can watch the car registration plates. NEG negative. ARG argument. Or argh (but argh is not a real word). BKL buckle. VVE revive. ELR – Yes, ELR elevator. DTF doubtful. NEW new. PEW phew. But maybe phew isn't a real word either. PEW periwinkle. Or just PEW pew. Good. The people on the gameshow on TV who have to do something like this, when Derek the Computer gives them the letters, don't win money, they win dictionaries or holidays at a health farm so it isn't really worth it. You know it is going to be a bad day on the days when you can't keep up with the letters going past on the cars.

Or you can choose to look up. Today the clouds are thick and unbroken though you don't think it will rain. Nuages. That was the French word for it at school. New ages, the sky full of them. It is nearly the end of the century. It is amazing how nearly the end of the century it is, you think, with your head back looking at the clouds. The end of the century will be a brilliant excuse for everybody to get really drunk and go really mad for a whole year. Or maybe two years, since it said in the paper once that they weren't sure which was the right year to celebrate the end of the century and the new age.

Clouds are particles of ice or water held in the air above ground level. You were good at geography. Cirrus, stratus, cumulus. They sound like magic words but in reality they are just the names of clouds. Cumulo-nimbus is like smoke. Cumulus-humilis, those are the ones like shreds of something in the sky, that can change their shape in seconds.

You watch them move above you, a mass of old grey wool.

It must be pretty good though, to work on this side of the road. Better than working on the other where you would never get the sun. Which is what the woman in the fruit shop said to you once, one day when it was sunny. You never get the sun on this side of the street. There is a song about that. It is quite good to think that thing about her having a face like bruised fruit, since she actually sells fruit. It looks like someone has really punched her. It particularly looks like someone has been hitting her, because she is pretending so hard that it doesn't matter, that she is just having a day at work, though she is avoiding the eyes of the people who buy things from her and refusing to smile back if they smile at her, and when anyone speaks to her, from the way she is holding herself, it looks as though she is frightened of their words. The pavement outside her shop is covered in boxes of withered-looking flowers. Some days she waves to you, but today you are careful not to look at her when she might see you looking. Her face is a nice face.

You see your own blank face flash before you twice on the shiny moving windows of a car. LFL lawful. SEG. AMR. UAV. TVK.

You watch the faces and clouds and keep your eye out for the words. Some words you get, others you don't.

Demands

What's your name? the old lady says.

Gayle, says Gayle.

You're not from round here, the old lady says.

No, I suppose that's right, I'm not, Gayle says, and laughs politely.

No, the old lady says. I knew you weren't.

The front door has a bell in the centre with a piece of paper heavily sellotaped over it. Below the sellotape are words: NOT WORKIN. Gayle follows the old lady through the house. The old lady is so small it is like following a small square child. It is hard to tell if it's that she's fat or if it's the number of layers of clothes she's wearing.

The smell of old things gets stronger as they go from room to room. There are photographs everywhere, some framed, some pinned, curling off the walls. In the first room they go through there are piles of clothes everywhere, and there is junk all over the back room, like a charity shop. It smells like a charity shop. Through the corridor the narrow cracked kitchen is all dishes and dirt, and smells of old animals. It's good of you to help me Gayle, the old lady is saying. Gayle tells her it's no bother at all. She is careful not to touch any surfaces.

Gayle, Gayle, the old lady says as she works at the back door with the key. It's a nice name that, Gayle. I can't do it any more, it's too big for me to move. And after you've taken it round, come back and I'll give you a piece of chocolate.

No no, Gayle says laughing, that won't be necessary. I mean I won't need a piece of chocolate. Don't you worry about any chocolate.

I used to work for a minister and his wife was called Gayle, the old lady says. He was a minister. I used to clean the house for them up Alpha Road. They were from Whitby. Have you heard of that Whitby? I used to like the sound of Whitby when I used to draw maps. Like Whitsun.

Was that what you used to do when you were young, map drawing? Gayle asks.

Oh yes, when I was a girl, I used to draw maps, the old lady says. She is breathless, still pushing and twisting her hands at the key in the door. There is a line of dirt like a bracelet round one of her wrists.

So where is it you want me to take it? Gayle asks. Shall I take it right round to the front door?

Panic crosses the old lady's face. Oh no, she says. Not right round to the front. I'll never get it back if you take it all the way round to the front. You just take it to the end of the lane. Then the men empty it. I can get it back if you just leave it at the end of the lane.

It'll be a lot easier when it's empty, Gayle says. The smell in the room is overpowering now. She puts her hands on her hips. Then she folds her arms with her hands tucked in.

D'you know, eh, Gayle, I can't get it open, the old lady says.

Here, let me try, Gayle says kindly.

The key gives and turns when Gayle puts her whole weight behind it. The door opens on to an overgrown garden with rubbish in the grass. There is a chicken carcass on the mat by the back door.

Christmas, the old lady says, and kicks it. Look, the birds have picked it clean. She laughs. Her laugh sounds like something falling and breaking.

I'll put that in the bin too, shall I? Gayle says. She picks up the thin-boned carcass between her thumb and her first finger. It is as light as air.

You're a good girl, Gayle, the old lady says. And then come back round for some chocolate.

Gayle tips the bin up on to its wheels. It is quite hard to push because of the grass being so tangled. A cloud of mosquitoes flies up out of the grass. Bye now, she shouts over her shoulder. Maybe see you again. She pretends she hasn't heard the bit about the chocolate.

So are you married, Gayle? the old lady calls from the back door.

Gayle keeps pushing the bin against the lawn. No, she calls back. Not yet.

You'll still be in school then, the old lady shouts. Her voice is high and frail.

Gayle laughs. I'm far too old for that, she calls back over the bin. No, I work in an office.

Oh, an office, the old lady says.

I work in the travel agent's on the Broadway, Gayle says. Do you know it?

Oh, that'll be good. All over the world, they go, the old lady says.

But I'm thinking of doing another course, Gayle says. To get qualifications. There are a lot of courses you can do.

Oh yes, the old lady says far away at the other end of the garden. You can do a lot of things these days, can't you, hotels or hospitals or anything.

Gayle opens the back gate. The wood of it is rotten.

My name's Marjory, the old woman is calling. She waves both her hands in the air at Gayle.

Goodbye, Gayle shouts, and waves back.

She pushes the bin up the lane and leaves it at the top by some other bins. She dusts down her hands. She looks at her watch. She has missed two buses.

On her way to the bus stop she passes a boy sitting in the doorway of the post office. He is wrapped in a blanket and there is a dog's head peeping out from beneath the edge. It is a puppy really rather than a dog. Gayle reaches down to pat its head.

He's called Charlie, the boy tells her.

He's lovely, Gayle says.

He's twelve weeks. He's just had his injections, the boy says.

Gayle gives him some money, keeping aside the change she needs for the bus. She doesn't usually give them money, because once she gave money to a man and then she noticed a syringe at his foot, and he saw her notice and tried to kick it out of the way but it was too late, and it was too late for her to get her money back.

She decides not to buy something to eat because she won't be able to eat it anyway until she gets home and washes her hands. She stands in the queue at the bus stop. Behind her, on all the tv screens in the second hand tv shop window, the African man is on the news again. It is a bit of a joke. Last night he was on the news when he arrived in Britain, because he had come to find the head of an old historic African he was related to, whose head he says was taken by British soldiers who cut off bits of it, like the ears and the lips, and made them into trophies, and put what was left of it in a museum. Everybody had been talking about it at work. He had arrived at Heathrow and had shaken a stick covered in feathers at the customs people. David at work thought it might put people off visiting Africa, which is a real winter moneyspinner and they couldn't afford that to happen at work. But Tony thought it would maybe make more people want to go, because of tradition.

Gayle thinks about her day. This morning she was in a very bad mood, but now she isn't at all. She thinks about the old lady and how she helped her. She tries to remember what the old lady looked like, but she can't. She can't even remember what the boy she's just given money to looks like, though she can remember what his dog's face is like. She looks along the bus queue. Then she shuts her eyes and tries to remember what the people look like and in what order. It is very difficult.

In her head the old lady's face shifts and changes. Her house changes. The smell goes, the dirt goes, the town and the time change, and Gayle is looking up at her grandmother, who is dead. But this is a long time before she died, and they are in the white-tiled bathroom in the new council house. Gayle is staying for the weekend. It is a real treat. Her grandmother is showing her how to do magic (it is in the days before fabric softener). She shows her how, if you put the bathroom light out when you're getting undressed to have your bath, and you pull your dress fast enough over your hair and your head, you can make sparks come from nowhere, you can feel the sting of them and if you're quick enough you can even see them round you in the dark.

Gayle smiles to herself. She has done at least two good turns today. She looks away so that no one in the bus queue will see her smiling at nothing. She feels good. She tells herself that probably nobody else in this bus queue today is feeling as good as she is.

Pictures

1: Women at Work in Jam Factory, circa 1948.

The rumour ran down the line at work, whispered from girl's mouth to girl's ear under the sound of the machines one June morning when the sun threw great slants of light across the machines and over the floor. No, it's true, listen. Why shouldn't it be, when they can send not just voices but pictures with no effort at all all the millions of miles across the world, and when something can happen like Annie Bradley's man walking in like he did after they all thought he was dead and gone, and turning Annie's hair from brown to white in one night? Have you not seen her? Completely white right down to the roots.

One girl knew someone who knew someone who had seen one of the pictures. She swore on it. The people in them lie about on clouds, with wisps of cloud all round their heads. This woman who had the picture bought it in a studio in London because she had seen her fiancé in it and he was a pilot and was dead, and there he was on a cloud with people all round him, and they were all smiling, though she didn't know any of the people he was with, and she wondered what he was doing with them, all strangers to her.

Grace Chambers laughed out loud when Margie told her it in her ear. I'll bleeding well swear on it too, she said. But she passed on the rumour to the next girl down the line; the next girl was waiting to hear.

Polly sent a note down the line to Margie. Margie tucked it inside her rolled-up sleeve to read when Bithell wouldn't catch her; she was already in trouble. Bithell was down on her for coming in late, it had been such a nice day. But Bithell said maybe Miss Stewart would like to be out in the sun and out of a job too and that this would be easily arrangeable.

Grace stood in front of her so Bithell couldn't see. Polly's note said: Can you get Saturday off? Margie left the line and went up to the glass box.

Who's covering for you on the line? Bithell asked without looking up.

Grace is, Miss Bithell, Margie said. Please, Miss Bithell, can I take Saturday off? A relative is sick and Grace Chambers says she'll work it for me.

Bithell stared at her until she shut the door and backed down the steps.

Measled old toad. Old bitch, face like a clothespeg, like old cheese rind, Margie said under her breath after she turned her back. But it was all right. It'd be all right. She'd written to the telephone exchange for a job. She'd written to a churchman about a housekeeping position. She wasn't going to spend her whole life with her hands bloody well red up to the elbows and stains all over her front and her face. Her hands would be as white as the girls in Labelling. That'd be the life. That'd be the life she'd be having.

2: Debris in Queen Street after bombing, September 1944.
3: Margie and Polly and Vera on the beach at Kings Lynn, Spring 1938.

On Friday night Margie left her blue dress out for Polly to wear to London next day. She pinned the note neatly to the front of it. *See if you see any person I knew and if you do get it I will get the money some how thanks your a love M.*

Do you think there are special rules for who gets to be in it? Margie said to Grace.

Heaven? Grace said. Christ. You bet there are.

No, Margie said. Do you think, like, people get their photo taken because they've just arrived? Do you think they have to share a cloud with people they don't even know? Or what if you ended up on the same cloud as her? Margie jerked her head. Above them Miss Bithell was watching the fruit rolling down the line to be crushed, watching that nobody was eating it.

She's already bought her ticket for her place on the same cloud as you, Grace said, and poked Margie in the side with her elbow. Nah, the likes of her have a special heaven, where they get glass boxes to sit in so they can masticate away to their hearts' content.

Grace had a filthy mouth because she'd gone out with Americans. When will Poll be back? she said. I want to see these pictures. I'd like to meet the man that took them. He'd be worth a bob or two so he would, he knows his way around the world and that's no lie.

Grace had lost all three sisters the night they blew half of Queen Street away.

4: Faked Picture of Heaven (circa 1947/8, now a collector's item, an auctionable rarity).

Polly brought back two pictures in the end. They were so small you could hardly see the faces, which were impossible to make out anyway. You could make out the smiling and not much else. The man and the woman who ran the studio where you could buy the pictures of heaven charged 2/6 each, and Polly said there was a sign up saying that they could maybe get one of a person you knew, if you could provide them with details of what the person looked like when he or she was alive. Polly and Margie actually thought about saving a bit of money and doing that, before it was in the papers that the police had shut the shop down and taken the man and the woman to court after someone who was still alive spotted herself dead in heaven in one of the pictures, and the papers said how the man and woman had been charged with fraud and that the man had been to prison after the last war for it too. The papers said they were fined. So that meant they were maybe still doing the pictures somewhere.

None of the faces looked like anyone they knew. Neither Margie nor Polly could recognise any of the people. Grace looked at the pictures and laughed out loud. The pictures got passed down the line with Polly nervous at the pulper, watching to make sure she'd get them back. But then some girl thought she knew someone in one of them, so Polly said she could have the picture, if she paid her the full 4/- for it.

5: Mother and dad, 1922.
6: Mother and dad and the girls, 1935.
7: Polly in the garden, 1967
8: Polly and Jack in the garden, don't know when.
9: Mary and Uncle Edward, 1930s.
10: Harold and Margie, 1977.
11: Trevor on Harold's side, 1994.
12: Margie's retirement do at the Labour club, 1982.

When Polly went, in 1977, the picture of heaven with its eight blurred faces looking out of the clouds got left with the rest of her stuff to Margie, her sister, who pinned it up on the wall with all the other photos.

13: Fifteen girls at work out the back having a smoke, 1949.

There's Polly. There's Margie. That one three along is Grace Chambers. It's not a good likeness. Margie can't remember all the other names now, all those girls at work back then.

14: Row of shops, 1997.
15: Bus queue, 1997.
16: Old lady asleep in chair with mouth open and television on, 1997.

Instructions for pictures of heaven

First, find a photograph of a crowd. It can be one you've taken yourself or one out of a newspaper. Newspaper is good, anonymous and ethereal. It is preferable to choose a happy-looking crowd, smiling faces: a football crowd or a new year crowd or a crowd at a hanging. Peace breaking out is good, or people waiting to cheer royalty on the balcony. Whichever, you will find you get best results from photographs taken from some distance and from above looking down.

Next, cut round some of the faces with a sharp blade. Choose faces that are poorly defined. Cut roughly around hats and hair. Cut round more than one face if you want; two or three can go down well, but be careful, and certainly don't use more than three. Remember, you risk revealing your original source.

Now fill a small clean tin tray with water. Suspend lens and lighting at angles directly above. Place the cut out faces on lumps of roughly torn wool. (Five or so of these lumps should fit comfortably, with ample space round them, into your tray.) Timing is crucial here, n.b..

Gently and swiftly place the wool on the water. (You may find it useful to ask someone to help with this part of the procedure.) Wait only the second or so it takes for the wool to have absorbed just enough and not too much of the water, enough to weight it still but before it soaks through and destroys the faces. This is the ideal moment to take your picture.

Develop your picture. Pin successful pictures in your window with wedding, engagement and family portraits and the portraits of babies and children. Prepare for your next photograph by returning to stage one (above). Meanwhile, outside your window, crowds will gather peering and pointing. You will hear the shop bell as they push the door open. In wartime particularly, it is guaranteed, you will make a fortune.

IRVINE WELSH

Dreaming of a White Christmas

Keasbo is sitting in an armchair in his dingy flat. It's cold –
very, very cold – but he's too skagged-up to notice. On the
couch Jackie, his girlfriend of however many days it was since
he came into a quality bit of gear, is starting to get strung out
in front of the telly. The Pope is on the box with a Christmas
message of peace.

– Hear that auld cunt: fuckin wanker. Aw they cunts, thir aw
fuckin wankers, Keasbo sneers.

– Needin mair skag Keasbo, eh . . . Jackie says, breathlessly,
shivering, realising that now the acknowledgement has been
made, the suffering will remorselessly rev up until her needs
will have to be met.

Keasbo can't hear her. He is still animated, as he tends to
be when he comes into some China White instead of the more
common brown. It's always his custom to mix it up with a bit of
speed. For some reason he never does this with the broon stuff.
That's Johnny Swan's way: he being the party whom Keasbo
has scored the white from.

As Jackie pleads, Keasbo continues scrutinising the Pope.
Fuckin cunt. A brief sectarian impulse flashes through his mind,
an old tape being replayed. But it isn't the one Keasbo is looking
for. He moves on and a vague recollection forms in his head
and quickly crystallises and spouts into a fully-fledged tale that
needs telling. – Did ah ever tell ye what happened when that
auld fucker went tae one ay they South American countries? He
gestures dismissively at the box, oblivious to Jackie's contorting

face. – The daft cunt goes ower tae these Indian punters fae this tribe, and these boys gie um a bound copy ay the bible wi an inscription in thair lingo, oan the fron ay it likes. So the auld wanker's aw chuffed until one ay his aides tells um what the inscription says: TAKE YOUR FUCKIN BOOK BACK. IT'S BROUGHT US NOTHING BUT POVERTY AND MISERY. Ha ha ha, Keasbo laughs coldly, the laughter of a guy with his mates rather than his bird, which he becomes aware of and which makes him feel a little uneasy, but he has started so he's finishing. – That's tellin they cunts. Ha ha ha.

Jackie is not impressed. She pulls some strands of long, greasy brown hair from her face and fastens them behind her ear where she hopes they will stay. The contact of her cold hand makes her ear throb and burn. She shudders again. – Skag Keasbo . . . ah'm sufferin here. Ah'm needin a fuckin fix, eh Keasbo . . .

Keasbo recognises that, although he isn't sick yet, Jackie's unremitting insistence on charting her own decline will inevitably precipitate his. He'd best get sorted soon, while he still can. It is Christmas Eve tomorrow. This means that everybody will be away. It always strikes him that the most unlikely people – dealers, junkies, wasters, whom he could never imagine sitting down to a turkey dinner with the family – did in fact, invariably vanish at this time of the year. He has a brief vision of Johnny Swan and Seeker topped by party hats pulling a cracker together, one all rotten teeth, the other a deadpan expression. The cracker splits apart like a flashbulb igniting and everyone is covered in white powder. – A white Christmas . . . he says softly to himself. Yes, everybody went to their families. Everybody except Keasbo. Not after the last time.

– Keith, c'moan! Jackie pleads.

– Aye, ah'm fucked n aw, he acknowledges. – Ye goat hirey's? He looks at her urgently, but more in hope than in expectation.

– Naw.

Keasbo feels a surge of anger. He is financing her habit as well as his own. What fuckin use was she? He hudnae even shagged her yet. The old holy papa's goat mair chance ay getting ehs hole than me, Keasbo thinks. Fuckin hell, a loat mair ay a chance given the shite ye read aboot Priest's cowpin everything in sight.

– Ah've burned every fucker doon. Swaney'll no let ays through the door n Seeker'll want cash up front. Huv tae hit ma sister, at that sheltered housing scheme, eh.

– Will she gie ye any money? Jackie asks, her face hard and eyes penetrating.

– Aye, course she will, Keasbo says emphatically, before realising that it's been a long time since he's seen Susan. Oh God, it was last Christmas and that had been the first time in three years, although he'd been inside before that. A prison sentence did that: stopped you getting out and about. Susan though, she'd never come and visit him back then. Just acted normal when he got out, like he had never been inside. Then last Christmas, at the auld man and auld lady's he'd fucked it up there alright. Fucked it in the service of junk. Here he was though, he was doing it again, resurrecting the ghosts of Christmas past. – Ah mean surely tae fuck aye, eh. Ah mean Christmas; time fir faimlay n aw that shite, he considers, trying to force resolve into his tone.

– Hurry then Keith, Jackie urges. She wants him right on the case and back with a result before all this gets too much. She bunches up in her chair, drawing her knees to her chest and crushing a threadbare cushion under her chin. The wait was ahead. Always the wait.

– Too right doll. Be a white Christmas eftir aw eh? Or a broon yin anywey. Keasbo looks searchingly at her again. Junk has blunted her looks and sexuality but sometimes a certain gesture or expression showed him where they had been. Aye, there's quality fanny lurking under the surface of this grey, sweating, bent figure and no mistake, he calculates. – Tell ye what . . . see whin ah git back . . . mibee a wee ride, eh Jackie? Keasbo ventures, experimenting more with his own reactions than hers. It's been a while since he's had sex. He'd gone in for it in a big way when he came back out the nick, but then he'd got back on the junk and it just faded into the background. He tried to attach some kind of value to it, first through the recall of sexual experiences, then via their absence, but it was like it had never happened for him. Never had it, never missed it, he thinks with a faint smile. Finding his libido was like trying to tune into a radio station with a poor signal and a terrible reception. If you concentrated hard enough and were deft enough you could occasionally pick it up, but it never lasted and was invariably drowned out by the other stations which surrounded it with their twenty-four hour blaring SKAG.

– Aye . . . right. Jist git the gear, Jackie says. The thought of Keasbo's cock inside her fills her with something staggering slowly towards the state of apathy.

Keasbo gets the message, not from her but from his pain centres which tingle in preparation for a more sustained onslaught. He hauls himself out of the armchair and leaves the room. In the lobby he puts on his old overcoat and takes a deep breath before heading out the door and down the stairs. Keasbo wants to build up a head of steam which will take him from the top of Leith Walk to Gorgie and back but as he emerges from the stair door into the street a group of young kids start pelting him with snowballs, shouting at him: – Junkie! Fuckin junkie!

– Fuckin wide wee cunts! Keasbo snaps, but without breaking his stride, still hurrying down the snowy pavement.

– Junkie, junkie, his baws urnae spunky . . . the kids sing in a malevolent rhyme.

Keasbo looks back at this. The kids had dug in closer to the bone that time. – Fuck off ya wee cunts! Ah'd fuckin shag everyone ay youse wee bastards tae death!

One snowball hits his shoulder and the cold water trickles down the inside of his collar. Keasbo shudders but he doesn't even attempt to give chase, he just carries on around the corner to the main road where he waits at the bus stop. Fortunately for him, he doesn't have to wait too long. The bus is trundling through the snow up the Walk. He gets on and sits in the disabled seat without even bothering to show the disinterested driver his out-of-date pass. The withdrawal is kicking in and he is shaking and feverish as the bus ambles towards the city centre.

The city goes past him and Keasbo is a bit disconcerted to note that he can't make out anything through the dirty windows of the bus and the white glare of snow, only the odd, darkened, smudge of a passer-by. It could be the fuckin North Pole ootside, he thinks. The bus turns sharply and he is pushed forward in his seat. Now though, he can recognise Haymarket and the narrow, main thoroughfare of Dalry Road. Once again Keasbo starts to think about shagging. Keasbo considers the city and thinks of all the places he like to put his cock: if Leith Walk is Edinburgh's giving, generous fanny, then Gorgie Road and Dalry Road are its arsehole, a long, tight-as-fuck shit-tube. He thinks this is a bit indulgent but he knows that he loves the city so much that one day he'd just like to take it to bed with him and fuck it every way.

Keasbo gets off the bus in Gorgie Road. He walks a little, slipping and almost falling over in the snow, but managing to correct himself. The cold is now biting, but he is more aware of his pulse playing strange rhythms in different parts of his body. His organic tissue feels saturated with toxins.

He comes upon a gleaming, granite new-build structure which is the sheltered housing complex, and he enters it through double doors. The rush of warm air from the central heating system and the sharp and stale smell of old bodies it carries blasts him. Striding down a long corridor Keasbo notes a dining room which is full of elderly people, seated around a set table.

Going next door to a substantial kitchen, he sees his sister Susan, red and sweaty as she lifts a tray of food out of a big oven onto a worktop. She is looking harassed, wearing oven gloves and an apron, and has still not noticed Keasbo.

–Eh Sooz, he says, slightly timidly. He has always been in some awe of his sister. She is five years older than him and has always epitomised straightness and organisation. He thinks of them as kids. She wasn't cruel, but she knew how to set him up for some hidings. Then again, he must have been a pain in the arse at times. And now here he was again. It was good not to grow up, but maybe sometimes you could not grow up in the wrong way. Life, he reflects, quickly smothering that maverick thought with a psychic blanket before it burned too deeply.

– Keith! Long time no see, Susan says, turning and seeming genuinely pleased to see him. Keasbo's anticipation level rises.
– Thank god n aw, she continues. His smile broadens. It's been a long time since the word 'Keith' preceeded the term 'Thank God', at least in his presence. – Look, ah'm up tae ma eyes in it here. Everybody else is oaf sick and ah'm huvin tae gie the auld folks their Christmas lunch. You can make yirself useful and serve the sherry.

She points to glasses of sherry stacked on a huge, oval-shaped silver tray before going back to the oven and producing a large turkey which she dumps on a table.

Keasbo's spirits have fallen. He looks at the silver tray, the glasses of sherry and then back at his sister. This won't do. Keasbo's here on urgent business, not to fanny about with auld cunts and their sherry. The concept strikes him as not so much alien as inappropriate. – Eh Sooz, um a bit short likesay . . .

Susan's not hearing him though. She picks up the sherry tray and moves towards him. – Christ ye look terrible. Huv you goat that flu virus n aw? she asks, trying to scrutinise beyond the wasted image that confronts her.

Keasbo shifts under that gaze of old. – Aye, it's a killer, he agrees, – Eh, ah forgoat tae go tae the bank . . . kin ye lend ays some dosh? Jist fir the morn.

– We'll see, she says, thrusting the tray at him, forcing him to take it, – but you've goat tae gie the auld yins their sherry! Ah'm up tae ma eyes in it! Aw hands tae the pump, she urges.

– Aye but . . . Keasbo protests in a biscuit-ersed manner. He feels himself eight years old again, trailing in her gum-chewing adolescent slipstream. She'd assumed a mantle of certainty in his eyes at that time, and had never let it slip since then.

–Take the tray through! Susan commands. – And some ay they auld yins kin be funny, so mind and serve it right!

Keasbo obeys without further questioning, though he's shaking as he finds himself going through the connecting doors into the dining room. The glasses seem to slide with each step he takes. The old folks stop their chatter and survey him in a disapproving silence. One woman with a twisted lower lip positively glowers.

Through his wretchedness and the hostile reception he receives, Keasbo struggles to affect a saccharine cheerfulness. – The sherry is served . . . he announces with as much of a grandiose flourish as he can manage.

The woman with the twisted lip turns to her neighbour and hisses, – Look at um Jessie, ehs shakin . . . ehs spillin aw the sherry . . .

Jessie, looking cold in spite of the thick woollen cardigan she is wearing, nods fervently and announces to the table in a high, shrill, indignant voice, – Eh cannae stoap bloody well shakin! The sherry's spillin! She points accusingly at Keasbo. Then she herself visibly shivers, as if the presence of this evil spirit is frosting over her bones.

But the sherry *is* spilling. Keasbo is oscillating on the spot. He just wants to dump the tray on the table so they can help themselves and he can fuck off, but not one of the old cunts is clearing a space for him, some of them have their fuckin handbags on it for fuck's sakes. But now he's more aware of it than ever before, the fact that he's sick, just so fuckin sick, he's trembling miserably and he sees the looks of hatred boring into him from the occupants of the table . . .

An old guy in a suit, one of only two men at the table, looks disgustedly at Keasbo, unshaven as he is and wrapped in his scabby old overcoat. – That bloody mess servin us oor Christmas din . . . he stutters as Keasbo tries to lower the tray to the table but loses control and the glasses slide off and topple like British soldiers at the Somme, spilling their blood-red contents all over Jessie and her neighbour.

– Oh my god! One woman shrieks, then bursts into tears.

– Look at um! Jessie's dress! He's bloody well ruined it! The woman with the lip shouts as Jessie hyperventilates.

Keasbo looks at the carnage on the table and then at the sea of lynch-mob faces. The cursing and moaning of the old folks becomes a background cacophony as he raises his gaze above their heads, focusing on a picture on the wall. It's Greyfriars Bobby, that wee dug, he thinks. Then he can sense his sister Susan running in and gasping and getting a cloth and ineffectively dabbing at sherry-soaked laps. He lowers his gaze. From the depths of his tormented soul he lets rip with an almighty roar, digging his elbows into his side to force out the angst as well as to stabilise himself – SHUT THE FUCK UP YA STUPID AULD CUNTS! YIS IR AW FUCKIN WELL GAUNNY BE DEID

SOON SO WHIT UR YIS FUCKIN WELL WORRYIN
ABOOT YA MINGIN AULD BASTARDS! AH HOPE IT'S
YIR LAST FUCKIN CHRISTMAS YA FUCKIN SMELLY
AULD CUNTS! NAE WONDER YIR FUCKIN FAIMLAYS
DIDNAE WANT YIS THIS CHRISTMAS! FUCK YIS! GIT
A FUCKIN WASH! A'HM OOT AY HERE. AH CANNAE
STAND THE SMELL AY PISH COMIN FAE YIS!

There is a brief silence. Keasbo suffused with a new energy,
turns on his heels and runs out of the complex down the road,
scarcely aware of the cold air.

Keith! What's wrong! What happened? What have ye done!
Susan has followed him and is shouting after him.

– You kin fuck off n aw! Jist fuck off! he turns and snaps at her,
flailing the air with the back of his hand. A startled man and
woman passing by quickly cross over to the other side of the
road. Susan stands rooted to the spot, bristling with indignation.
She then turns and runs back into the complex, holding her
jacket together with one hand, her free arm swinging stiffly, as
if operating like a rudder as she heads to her destination.

Keasbo's spirits dip. He realises that he has come away
empty-handed. As soon as this thought sinks home, he is
moving with the same purpose, but back in the direction he
just came from. – Sooz! Ah'm sorry Sooz! he pleads, running
after her. He bangs on the glass doors of the complex which
Susan has locked behind her. She is facing him sternly through
the glass. – Ah sais ah wis sorry . . . he implores.

– You git away fae here Keith Halcrow or ah'll phone the polis
masel! See if a willnae!

– Jist gies a score Sooz! Fir Christmas n that! Goan! Keasbo begs,
– GO-OH-OHNN! he beseeches her, but Susan is unyielding.
She then moves out of his vision and she is replaced by a pack
of scornful malevolent old faces.

– CUNTS! Keasbo shouts. – FUCKIN CUNTS!

Then it hits him that Susan may very well be going to phone the police, so he legs it back down the road.

Keasbo rushes down the street for a few yards, his mind buzzing and his body feeling sick and twisted. Sitting down and trembling on a cold park bench, he wraps his arms around himself and tries to gather his thoughts. Then in a surge of inspiration he realises that his brother Gary lives within walking distance at Harrison Gardens.

Gary, though, represents an even worse bet than Susan, he thinks to himself. We dinnae get oan. The cunt willnae even let ays in the fuckin hoose. He's probably no even in anywey. Keasbo's considering all this while at the same time heading as fast as his legs can take him in the direction of Harrison Gardens. No, they didn't get on, but it was Christmas. Gary would surely be good for a double score.

Gary is in. His face falls with the same level of elasticity that serves to snap Keasbo's into a crinkle of a smile when the siblings confront each other on the doorstep. – Keith . . . eh, come in . . .

– Gaz, Keasbo nods, walking past him into the flat and heading for the front room.

– How ye daein? Gary says, trying to battle against the resignation in his voice.

– No bad . . . eh, jist daein a wee bit ay Christmas visitin . . . been doon the road tae see Sooz n that, ken it the sheltered housin?

Gary looks at him for a second, then shakes his head miserably. – Yir no back oan that shite again, are ye?

– Naw, ah jist thought wi it bein Christmas . . .

– Aye right, Gary snaps. – Dinnae you be gaun roond tae ma Ma's. Right? Ah'm fuckin well warning ye. She disnae need that shite oafay you again!

200

Keasbo looks at his brother. It irritates him how he appropriates their parents in that way, excluding him. But he couldn't bullshit Gary. While Susan ignores his condition, Gary was invariably straight to the point. Too fuckin straight to the point, Keasbo thinks, too fuckin eager to emphasise the difference between them. – Look, ah need some dough for Christmas. Ah'm skint . . . ah jist thought . . .

Gary considers breaking into a lecture, one he prepares in his head about once a week, but as he has delivered it so many times before, he knows that it will do no good. Yvonne would be back from work soon and she would flip if she found this fucker here. The priority therefore was to get him out of the house, but keep him away from Ma's. There was only one way to do it and that way involved no gain to him. – Much dae ye need? he asks wearily.

– A ton, Keasbo ventures assertively, his junkie's mercenary understanding of the power dynamics between them honed to perfection. Gary had blown it when he'd mentioned their Ma.

– Eh! It's fuckin Christmas Keith!

– Ah widnae ask but . . .

– Aw right! But ah'm gaunny have tae go tae the cashpoint, Gary says sulkily.

Keasbo feels a massive surge of elation. – Ah'll chum ye! he volunteers with enthusiasm.

– Naw, you'll have tae stey here wi the bairn, Gary warily states, gesturing him to come into the kitchen. A toddler in a high chair was pushing a spoon around a bowl of food. It's Keasbo's niece, and he's only seen her once before.

– Hiya doll, mind ay me? Uncle Keith? he asks in a cold and brisk manner. Keasbo thinks about this for a split second, and is almost embarrassed at the difference between what he said and how it came out. The child just looks at him quizzically.

– You mind ay yir Uncle Keith! Course ye do.

Gary smiles coffin-plate style and then steals a doubtful look at his brother before ruffling his daughter's fine hair. He feels an internal twinge of fear then hate at the recognition that they are both his flesh. Shuddering inside he feels the possibility of all his unspoken ambitions for his child crash against the wasted rock that is his brother. Yet it is his brother. That has to count for something, though at this stage Gary can't think what.

– Ah want ma puddin. The little girl says.

– Gie her her sweet, Gary instructs Keasbo. – It's in the fridge. He shakes his head again, and kisses the little girl. – Back in a minute Princess, he says, pulling on a quilted jacket and heading out. – See she eats it, he adds as he departs.

More fuckin servitude, Keasbo thinks anxiously, but he can't really complain. – Now whaire's that sweet, Keasbo wonders out loud, looking at the fridge. There are magnets stuck on the front of it. They're offensively tacky and bright and this is a different world. He's feeling ugly and ill. He opens up, and inside the fridge there's a chocolate dessert in a bowl. It's sprinkled with hundreds and thousands.

His hands still trembling, Keasbo brings it over to his niece and sits down beside her. He takes a spoonful of dessert and holds it up to the child. It quivers. – Gaunny eat this? he almost pleads.

The child shakes her head slowly, emphatically and negatively. – Dinnae like they bits, she says, pointing at the yellow hundred and thousands with distaste.

– Fuck, Keasbo curses softly.

– Take them away! The little girl commands.

Keasbo starts to use the edge of the spoon to extract the yellow hundreds and thousands from the dessert, but his hand is shaky and some of the red and pink and blue ones come off as well. The child watches every move intently.

– Keep them! Keep the red! she screeches in horror.

– Fuckin wee bastard . . . ah'll fuckin . . . Keasbo tightens his grip on the spoon, twisting it into the dessert and wilfully stirring it into a pulp. – THERE'S YIR DESSERT YA FUCKIN SPOILT WEE BASTARD!

He springs from the table as the child's lungs explode into a long, ragged scream. Keasbo can't handle this. He storms out of the flat and into the stairwell. As he is heading down the stair, his brother is on his way back and they meet face on.

– Keith, Gary says in shock, – what's the fuckin score! Ye left the bairn oan her ain! Ye left the fuckin bairn!

– Naw Gaz, naw, the bairn's sound. A jist felt a wee bit dizzy . . . needed some air . . . ye goat the hirey's?

Gary shakes his head in slow disgust. Keasbo says nothing, as his brother looks at him in a hurt, bewildered way. – Ye wir gaunny leave the bairn! he whimpers.

Keasbo stays silent, letting Gary maintain his look of loathing and betrayal as he pulls out the wad. Keasbo attempts to look suitably ashamed as his brother hands the money over. Gary would expect it. Later, the shame would be real, but right now junk need has expunged it from his emotional vocabulary. All he can think about is the journey back to Leith and Seeker's China White. – Cheers Gaz, he says, and is already bouncing down the steps before his brother can respond. – Merry Christmas, Keasbo shouts into the stairwell without looking back or breaking his stride.

Getting out into the street he crosses over the footbridge at Slateford Road and runs down the steps and along Stewart Terrace. He sees the gleaming new stands of Tynecastle Park poking up beyond the sandblasted tenements.

Keasbo is now feeling as rough as fuck, but he is euphoric at having scored the dough. He's waiting as patiently as his throbbing cells will allow for the bus, right outside the Hearts football ground. One end is open and you can see right across the park into the new stands.

An old guy at the bus stop looks at him. – Thir supposed tae be buildin another yin at this side ay the groond. Ah've pit in ma complaint tae the council, cause ah stey in that tenement up thair, he says, pointing at the flats above them. – Thirty-two years. The best view ay the game. Baith goals n four corners ay the pitch. Now they want tae obstruct ma view by buildin a bloody stand right ootside ma kitchen!

– Fuckin nerve, eh?

– Aye, too right, the old guy nods.

Keasbo has had enough of old cunts for one day. He can see the bus coming up ahead. This auld fucker was getting it tight. – Ah dinnae ken what the world's comin tae, he says, malevolence rising inside him, – a fitba club wantin tae provide decent facilities tae paying customers, selfishly disregardin the rights ay a moochin auld jakey cunt who's hud thousands ay quid worth ay free fitba fir thirty-five years. It's sad eh? He says, striding from the curb to meet the advancing bus.

– Fuck off ya cheeky wee bastard! Ah'm entitled tae ma rights! The old guy barks. – Ah ken the score!

Keasbo laughs and puts his money in the box on the bus. He turns back and gives the old guy the V-sign. – Merry Christmas ya fuckin auld tube n ah hope yir next shite's a hedgehog!

As Keasbo takes his seat at the back of the bus, he notes that the snow is falling heavily – Leith driver, he says softly to himself, in an arrogant public-school accent, then smirks. – It's gaunny be a white Christmas right enough, he nods to a woman with a formidable pile of shopping who is sitting across from him.

– Looks like it, she smiles cheerfully.

– Surein it is, Keasbo laughs, giving the wad in his jeans pocket a reassuring tap.

JOHN ABERDEIN

Scone o Destiny

It wis Scone o Destiny day. Some hyped-up scone, bakit bi Jacob, ramfu o E's, *as hard as Abraham's* the babblers said, had gane the roonds, Egypt, Erin, Perth-wey, England, an wis langdue noo to process in the Leal Landrover tae its richtfu hame, the Castle-Forenenst-Jenners, sune as ye culd say *poprivettit perspex*. Micro-Forsyth had gotten ees inside leg measurit for a kilt, the Scots-at-Graze were paddlin up an doon on their fite horses, an Andra wis Princekin Squarrjaa, nivver wid Fergie's Crimsie Tae™ be galshach for that sturdy moo. It wis a fine fool day, the myths had cleart, blue sky an lashin rain.

Verry wis bein a set o tastebuds *Capuccino, Hanks?* jist eftir Ah'd cornert a perch at the cauld damp railins for hir. Betimes she wis baith bonny an fine, betimes gey snappach.

Uhuh, okay darl Ah says. *Nae ivvery day we're up the Mile.* Verry wis the thinkin man's rowie, she widna tak no for a placebo.

Hiv ye nae rowies? Ah says tae the waitress lass wi the pad an peenie.

Sir, sorry? Barely in Embra twa oors, already knichtit Laird o the Sorras.

Ah said rowies, hiv ye nane? R-O-W-E-E-Z, rowiesquery. Got ony in the day?

Scoanheid! says Verry *A'll dae thi askin. Croissants Pleins a la*

Dorique? she spiers the quine, settlit for muffin starters, het, an geelit beurre, wee VATvats o brandit jam.

Naebuddy said nithin.

Hanks?
Fit?
Thi Mental Leith A wander thll be uptoon thi day? gaes Verry, reid hair like Medusa wi that thirty-pound perm.
Wi their notebuiks? Ah says. *Eddie Claahemmir Gets His; Stanespottin; Three Pukes for Hir Radgesty – Heek! hup! hower aa!*
Aye ach A wander says Verry, menacin hir muffin wi a combat teaspune. *S ahappenin noo eh Scotlit but.*
Ihih Ah nods ma heid *Guid news earlier the month an aa.*
Wha?
The Wife o Usher's well.

Fucker ne spowk pas.

We hadna a brass meck atween us. Verry orderit hamecake n coffee, capuccino, hir lips froth-broon as an official historian's.
Kiss, aye? she pouts, ironic, very.
Ah luiks at hir. Times a sun-smile, afttimes stare-rods. Ah think Ah wis nae mair than a signed napkin till'r by this time.
Fond kiss? Ah says.
Naw an aa, Hunky-Door. Jist feel we shudna rendez fir a langish spell, guid while but. Did not *go fir wha-cam-ups last nicht!*
Ihih, Uhuh. Aye thocht ye were a guidwhile girl. An Ah'm the gallus laddie. Kennin foo rare confection turns its hert tae fuckt-up stane. *Let's gie it the sivven centuries then* Ah says. *That dae ye?* Trouble wis the nicht afore, wi visions picklin

ower me. Ah culdna tell the sheen o hir erse fae a chandelier. She sune tellt us tho.

We luikit past each ither, tae the best an first o wir time.

Bugger, let's gae gaes Verry, kidnappin the last o Cafe Muffin's Rowan Slice in a Mansize Scottie, they were that busy bein St Andra's Day, the Stane an aa.

Missit, of coorse we had, the hale procession, the croods were stamperin awa. Alaft on the prissy ramparts the fusiliers were giein it the twenty-one bangs ootower the Firth o Greymooth, as HMS *Newcastle* focht back wi pluffs o smowk.

The Snappach tuik us up this mochie close *Come oan!* hir hair aa booncin cheery. Ah culd feel hir saft an warm inside hir coat. An ae-gun salute wis guid eneuch for us an aff she went.

Jobby Numbers

1 U-Boats. Aa the wey up tae Archangel ee wis shitin himsel fir U-boats. At midnicht they wid be hackin ysh aff the steel railins fan somebuddy wid drap an aix, claang.

2 CLAANG! Jobby wid flee intae that wee deck-lavvy wi ees hert gaain clapclapclap like a feartie, feart o the mine-clunk, the torpedo's dirl.

3 Eftir, fan ee wis inower the raft wi the padre, the muckle swall hissan past them in the dark, the raft lollopin up an doon like an auld dune hoor, they cuddlit thegither for the affa cauld.

4 He thocht the padre hid a hard-on, an wis faain in luve wi'm. Bit fan the mannie faintit, an ees phiss gaed geelt, Jobby Numbers pit ees haun doon tae see fit wis fit.

5 Hiddlit deep in the padre's greatcoat pooch wis a buik. Yleclaith covers. Jobby gruppit it oot. A *Holy Bible!* Aa o a suddent, under the full o the mune there wir snaa-hills rearin aa roon, but the raft's flet erse was for whooshan them doon, doon tae the boddom in bree an grue.

6 A sair sooch tae climm anither, but Jobby wi ae hoof got rid o the padre an the raft bobbit fine, gled o the less wecht.

7 Jobby Numbers read like mad. Ees een wir glued tae the *Bible* but the pages got spumy, sipan.

8 *Genesis* sune floodit, an *Exodus* got the chuck, ower the side in a sotter, jist as twa waves partit tae the reid sword o dawnin. An he saa a pink-gray corvette curvin awards'm, some chariot, on cogglie wheels. Jobby nivver said doo's egg.

9 Aa the wey back in the sick-bay hammock ee nivver lat go o ees *Bible* avaa, ee pillowed it, oxtered it, ate ees piece aff it.

10 Fanivver ee opened it, it wis like seein a slush-swall comin tae brak ower ees heid, aince again. Een flasht like a Leica, an wid nivver forget.

11 Some ither survivors, Bleck Jock, ravin McTavish, Mealy Jerker an Ae Ba, chored their pages in turn aff Jobby fir rollin a smowk. *Jist the ticket* said Ae Ba, settin a spunk till't.

12 Nae muckle sacrifice. Jobby, tho he spowk nithin tae naebuddy, mindit ivvery wird ee saa. As they came in the lenth o Leith, wi shrapnel in the Captain's chist, an a bomb-hole throu their deckin, Jobby hid jist wipit ees dock on the last page o *Revelation*.

13 Years eftir, in the East End o toon, Jobby wid come hurlin roon wi a hackit pram, pittan ees haun doon in buckets

for auld fox-furs, het-wattir pigs or duntit kettles, tae hawk for a tanner tae Cocky Hunter. O the raft, the padre an the frozen mune, Jobby nivver lat dab.

14 But on a simmer's day ye culd aften find'm sittan oot on ees mither's granite steps in Jasmine Terrace. Must've been saft granite, Peem thocht, it wis worn bumholla.

15 Peem mindit Jobby Numbers in aa ees regalia: bleck duffler, balaclava, an a pair o rubber gas-boots wi reid-ribbit taes. Kids sat roon'm, shoutit at'm an daunsit up an doon wi tugs on the railins.

16 Ae day Starry shoutit *Job Jobby. Job Jobby.*

17 Stracht back cam Jobby:

> *Yea, young children despised me;*
> *I arose, and they spake against me.*

18 Syne Iris spiert *Div ye ken ony mair, Jobby?*

19 An Jobby thocht she said *Job, eh?* an he answerit an said

> *But Job answered and said,*
> *Hear diligently my speech, and let this be your*
> *consolations.*
> *Suffer me that I may speak; and after that I*
> *have spoken, mock on.*
> *As for me, is my complaint to man? And if it*
> *were so, why should not my spirit be troubled?*
> *Mark me, and be astonished, and lay your hand*
> *upon your mouth.*
> *Even when I remember I am afraid, and*
> *trembling taketh hold on my flesh.*
> *Wherefore do the wicked live, become old, yea,*
> *are mighty in power?*

20   The kids were fidgettin an futrettin at that, sae Peem tried ane o the rude anes. Ah'll bet ye dinna ken the stert o *Numbers 25*.

21   Numbers himsel jist reelt it aff

> *And Israel abode in Shittim, and the people*
> *began to commit whoredom with the daughters*
> *of Moab.*
> *And they called the people unto the sacrifices of*
> *their gods; and the people did eat and bowed*
> *down to their gods.*
> *And Israel joined himself unto Baal-Peor: and*
> *the anger of the Lord was kindled against Israel.*
> *And the Lord said unto Moses, Take all the*
> *heads of the people, and hang them up before*
> *the Lord in the sun . . .*

22   *Woe, woe,* said Peem *ye're lang past the good bittie! Noo Sacont Kings!*

23   Nivver mindit did Jobby, better nor ony bingo, ye culd shout ony number, it wis aa ane tae him, the wee catechists culd caper, but nivver catch'm oot. He culd hiv bin on the wireless, tap o the bill at the Tivoli.

24   Ae day Raymie askit fit ee likit best in the War. *Go on, Jobby, tell us, fit did ye like best in the War?* Jobby sniffit, sniffit again, an stertit tae greet.

25   Ye hidna a job. Ye were saft in the heid, wi an affa fool smell. Ye went back in the hoose fan the sun went awa.

LEILA ABOULELA

The Museum

At first Shadia was afraid to ask him for his notes. The ear-ring made her afraid. And the straight long hair that he tied up with a rubber band. She had never seen a man with an ear-ring and such long hair. But then she had never known such cold, so much rain. His silver ear-ring was the strangeness of the West – another culture shock. She stared at it during classes, her eyes straying from the white scribbles on the board. Most times she could hardly understand anything. Only the notation was familiar. But how did it all fit together? How did *this* formula lead to *this*? Her ignorance and the impending exams were horrors she wanted to escape. His long hair, a dull colour between yellow and brown, different shades, it reminded her of a doll she had when she was young. She had spent hours combing that doll's hair, stroking it. She had longed for such straight hair. When she went to Paradise she would have hair like that. When she ran it would fly behind her. If she bent her head down it would fall over like silk and sweep the flowers on the grass. She watched his pony-tail move as he wrote and then looked up at the board. She pictured her doll, vivid suddenly after many years, and felt sick that she was day-dreaming in class, not learning a thing.

The first days of term, when the classes started for the MSc. in Statistics, she was like someone tossed around by monstrous waves. Battered, as she lost her way to the different lecture rooms, fumbled with the photo-copying machine, could not find anything in the library. She could scarcely hear or eat or see. Her eyes bulged with fright, watered from the cold. The course required a certain background, a background she didn't have. So she floundered, she and the other African students, the two Turkish girls, and the men from Brunei. As this collection from the Third World whispered their anxieties in grim Scottish corridors, the girls in nervous giggles, Asafa, the short, round-faced Ethiopian, said, in his grave voice, 'Last year, last year a Nigerian on this very same course committed suicide. *Cut his wrists.*'

Us and them, she thought. The ones who would do well, the ones who would crawl and sweat and barely pass. Two pre-determined groups. Asafa, generous and wise (he was the oldest) leaned and whispered to Shadia, 'The Spanish girl is good. Very good'. His eyes bulged redder than Shadia's. He cushioned his fears every night in the university pub; she only cried. Their countries were next-door neighbours but he had never been to Sudan, and Shadia had never been to Ethiopia. 'But we meet in Aberdeen!' she had shrieked when this information was exchanged, giggling furiously. Collective fear had its euphoria.

'That boy Bryan,' said Asafa, 'is excellent.'

'The one with the ear-ring?'

Asafa laughed and touched his own unadorned ear. 'The ear-ring doesn't mean anything. He'll get the Distinction. He did his under-graduate here, got First Class Honours. That gives him an advantage. He knows all the lecturers, he knows the system.'

So the idea occurred to her of asking Bryan for the notes of his graduate year. If she strengthened her background in stochastic processes and time series, she would be better able to cope with the new material they were bombarded with every day. She watched him to try to judge if he was approachable. Next to the courteous Malaysian students, he was devoid of manners.

212

He mumbled and slouched and did not speak with respect to the lecturers. He spoke to them as if they were his equal. And he did silly things. When he wanted to throw a piece of paper in the bin, he squashed it into a ball and aimed it at the bin from where he was sitting. If he missed, he muttered under his breath. She thought that he was immature. But he was the only one who was sailing through the course.

The glossy handbook for overseas students had explained about the 'famous British reserve' and hinted that they should be grateful, things were worse further south, less 'hospitable'. In the cafeteria, drinking coffee with Asafa and the others, the picture of 'hospitable Scotland' was something different. Badr, the Malaysian, blinked and whispered, 'Yesterday our windows got smashed, my wife today is afraid to go out.'

'Thieves?' asked Shadia, her eyes wider than anyone else's.

'Racists,' said the Turkish girl, her lipstick chic, the word tripping out like silver, like ice.

Wisdom from Asafa, muted, before the collective silence, 'These people think they own the world . . .' And around them the aura of the dead Nigerian student. They were ashamed of that brother they had never seen. He had weakened, caved in. In the cafeteria, Bryan never sat with them. They never sat with him. He sat alone, sometimes reading the local paper. When Shadia walked in front of him he didn't smile. 'These people are strange . . . One day they greet you, the next day they don't . . .'

On Friday afternoon, as everyone was ready to leave the room after Linear Models, she gathered her courage and spoke to Bryan. He had spots on his chin and forehead, was taller than her, restless, as if he was in a hurry to go somewhere else. He put his calculator back in its case, his pen in his pocket. She asked him for his notes and his blue eyes behind his glasses took on the blankest look she had ever seen in her life. What was all the

213

surprise for? Did he think she was an insect, was he surprised
that she could speak?

A mumble for a reply, words strung together. So taken
aback, he was. He pushed his chair back under the table with
his foot.

'Pardon?'

He slowed down, separated each word, 'Ah'll have them for
ye on Monday.'

'Thank you.' She spoke English better than him! How
pathetic. The whole of him was pathetic. He wore the same
shirt every blessed day. Grey stripes and white.

On the weekends, Shadia never went out of the halls and, unless
someone telephoned long-distance from home, she spoke to
no one. There was time to remember Thursday nights in
Khartoum, a wedding to go to with Fareed, driving in his
red Mercedes. Or the club with her sisters. Sitting by the
pool drinking lemonade with ice, the waiters all dressed in
white. Sometimes people swam at night, dived in the water,
dark like the sky above. Here, in this country's weekend of
Saturday and Sunday, Shadia washed her clothes and her hair.
Her hair depressed her. The damp weather made it frizz up
after she straightened it with hot tongs. So she had given up
and now wore it in a bun all the time, tightly pulled back away
from her face, the curls held down by pins and Vaseline Tonic.
She didn't like this style, her corrugated hair, and in the mirror
her eyes looked too large. The mirror in the public bathroom, at
the end of the corridor to her room, had printed on it 'This is the
face of someone with HIV'. She had written about this mirror to
her sister, something foreign and sensational, like hail and cars
driving on the left. But she hadn't written that the mirror made
her feel as if she had left her looks behind in Khartoum.

On the weekends, she made a list of money she had spent,

214

the sterling enough to keep a family alive back home. Yet she might fail her exams after all that expense, have to go back home empty-handed without a degree. Guilt was cold like the fog of this city. It came from everywhere. One day she forgot to pray in the morning. She reached the bus-stop and then realised that she hadn't prayed. That morning folded out like the nightmare she sometimes had, of discovering that she had gone out into the street without any clothes.

In the evening, when she was staring at multi-dimensional scaling, the telephone in the hall rang. She ran to answer it. Fareed's cheerful greeting. 'Here Shadia, Mama and the girls want to speak to you.' His mother's endearments, 'They say it's so cold where you are . . .'

Shadia was engaged to Fareed. Fareed was a package that came with the 7Up franchise, the paper factory, the big house he was building, his sisters and widowed mother. Shadia was going to marry them all. She was going to be happy and make her mother happy. Her mother deserved some happiness after the misfortunes of her life. A husband who left her for another woman. Six girls to bring up. People felt sorry for her mother. Six girls to educate and marry off. But your Lord is generous: each of the girls, it was often said, was lovelier than the other. They were clever too: dentist, pharmacist, architect, and all with the best of manners.

'We are just back from looking at the house.' Fareed's turn again to talk, 'It's coming along fine, they're putting the tiles down . . .'

'That's good, that's good,' her voice strange from not talking to anyone all day.

'The bathroom suites. If I get them all the same colour for us and the girls and Mama, I could get them on a discount. Blue, the girls are in favour of blue,' his voice echoed from one continent to another. Miles and miles.

'Blue is nice. Yes, better get them all the same clour.' He was building a block of flats, not a house. The ground-floor flat for his mother and the girls until they married, the first floor for him and Shadia. The girls' flats on the two top floors would be rented out. When Shadia had first got engaged to Fareed, he was the son of a rich man. A man with the franchise for 7Up and the paper factory which had a monopoly in ladies' sanitary towels. Fareed's sisters never had to buy sanitary towels; their house was abundant with boxes of *Pinky*, fresh from the production line. But Fareed's father died of an unexpected heart attack soon after the engagement party (five hundred guests at the Hilton). Now Shadia was going to marry the rich man himself. You are a lucky, lucky girl, her mother said and Shadia rubbed soap in her eyes so that Fareed would think she had been weeping about his father's death.

There was no time to talk about her course on the telephone, no space for her anxieties. Fareed was not interested in her studies. He had said, 'I am very broad-minded to allow you to study abroad. Other men would not have put up with this . . .' It was her mother who was keen for her to study, to get a post-graduate degree from Britain and then have a career after she got married. 'This way,' her mother had said, 'you will have your in-law's respect. They have money but you will have a degree. Don't end up like me. I left my education to marry your father and now . . .' Many conversations ended with her mother bitter, with her mother saying, 'No one suffers like I suffer,' and making Shadia droop. At night her mother sobbed in her sleep, noises that woke Shadia and her sisters.

No, on the long-distance line, there was no space for her worries. Talk abut the Scottish weather. Picture Fareed, generously perspiring, his stomach straining the buttons of his shirt. Often she had nagged him to lose weight but with no success. His mother's food was too good, his sisters were both overweight.

On the long-distance line listen to the Khartoum gossip as if listening to a radio play.

On Monday, without saying anything, Bryan slid two folders across the table towards her as if he did not want to come near her, did not want to talk to her. She wanted to say, 'I won't take them till you hand them to me politely.' But smarting, she said, 'Thank you very much.' *She* had manners. *She* was well brought up.

Back in her room, at her desk, the clearest handwriting she had ever seen. Sparse on the pages, clean. Clear and rounded like a child's, the tidiest notes. She cried over them, wept for no reason. She cried until she wetted one of the pages, stained the ink, blurred one of the formulas. She dabbed at it with a tissue but the paper flaked and became transparent. Should she apologize about the stain, say that she was drinking water, say that it was rain? Or should she just keep quiet, hope he wouldn't notice? She chided herself for all that concern. *He* wasn't concerned about wearing the same shirt every day. She was giving him too much attention – thinking about him. He was just an immature and closed-in sort of character. He probably came from a small town, his parents were probably poor, low-class. In Khartoum, she never mixed with people like that. Her mother liked her to be friends with people who were higher up. How else were she and her sisters going to marry well? She must study the notes and stop crying over this boy's handwriting. His handwriting had nothing to do with her, nothing to do with her at all.

Understanding after not understanding is fog lifting, pictures swinging into focus, missing pieces slotting into place. It is fragments gelling, a sound, vivid whole, a basis to build on. His notes were the knowledge she needed, the gaps filled. She struggled through them, not skimming them with the carelessness of incomprehension, but taking them in, making them a part of her, until in the depth of concentration, in the late hours of the nights, she lost awareness of time and place and, at last, when she slept she became epsilon and gamma and she became a variable making her way through discrete space from state i to state j.

It felt natural to talk to him. As if now that she had spent hours and days with his handwriting, she knew him in some way. She forgot the offence she had taken when he had slid his folders across the table to her, all the times he didn't say hello.

In the computer room, at the end of the statistical packages class, she went to him and said, 'Thanks for the notes. They are really good. I think I might not fail, after all. I might have a chance to pass.' Her eyes were dry from all the nights she had stayed up. She was tired and grateful.

He nodded and they spoke a little about the Poisson distribution, queuing theory. Everything was clear in his mind, his brain was a clear pane of glass where all the concepts were written out boldly and neatly. Today he seemed more at ease talking to her, though he still shifted about from foot to foot, avoided her eyes.

He said, 'Do ye want to go for a coffee?'

She looked up at him. He was tall and she was not used to speaking to people with blue eyes. Then she made a mistake. Perhaps because she had been up late last night, she made that mistake. Perhaps there were other reasons for that mistake. The mistake of shifting from one level to another.

She said, 'I don't like your ear-ring.'

The expression in his eyes, a focusing, no longer shifting away. He lifted his hand to his ear and tugged the ear-ring off. His earlobe without the silver looked red and scarred.

She giggled because she was afraid, because he wasn't smiling, wasn't saying anything. She covered her mouth with her hand then wiped her forehead and eyes. A mistake was made and it was too late to go back. She plunged ahead, careless now, reckless, 'I don't like your long hair.'

He turned and walked away.

The next morning, Multivariate Analysis, and she came in late, dishevelled from running and the rain. The professor whose name she wasn't sure of (there were three who were Mc something), smiled unperturbed. All the lecturers were relaxed and urbane, in tweed jackets and polished shoes. Sometimes she wondered how the incoherent Bryan, if he did pursue an academic career, was going to transform himself into a professor like that. But it was none of her business.

Like most of the other students, she sat in the same seat in every class. Bryan sat a row ahead which was why she could always look at his hair. But he had cut it: there was no pony-tail today! Just his neck and the collar of the grey and white striped shirt.

Notes to take down. *In discrimination analysis, a linear combination of variables serves as the basis for assigning cases to groups.*

She was made up of layers. Somewhere inside, deep inside, under the crust of vanity, in the untampered-with essence, she would glow and be in awe, and be humble and think, this is just for me, he cut his hair for me. But there were other layers, bolder, more to the surface. Giggling. Wanting to catch hold of a friend. Guess what? You wouldn't *believe* what this idiot did!

Find a weighted average of variables . . . The weights are estimated so that they result in the best separation between the groups.

After the class he came over and said very seriously, without a smile, 'Ah've cut my hair.'

A part of her hollered with laughter, sang, you stupid boy, you stupid boy, I can see that, can't I?

She said, 'It looks nice.' She said the wrong thing and her face felt hot and she made herself look away so that she would not know his reaction. It was true though, he did look nice, he looked decent now.

She should have said to Bryan, when they first held their coffee mugs in their hands and were searching for an empty table, 'Let's sit with Asafa and the others.' Mistakes follow mistakes. Across the cafeteria, the Turkish girl saw them together and raised her perfect eyebrows, Badr met Shadia's eyes and quickly looked away. Shadia looked at Bryan and he was different, different without the ear-ring and the pony-tail, transformed in some way. If he would put lemon juice on his spots . . . but it was none of her business. Maybe the boys who smashed Badr's windows looked like Bryan, but with fiercer eyes, no glasses. She must push him away from her. She must make him dislike her.

He asked her where she came from and when she replied, he said, 'Where's that?'

'Africa,' with sarcasm, 'Do you know where *that* is?'

His nose and cheeks under the rim of his glasses, went red. Good, she thought, good. He will leave me now in peace.

He said, 'Ah know Sudan is in Africa, I meant where exactly in Africa.'

'North-east, south of Egypt. Where are *you* from?'

'Peterhead. It's north of here. By the sea.'

It was hard to believe that there was anything north of Aberdeen. It seemed to her that they were on the northernmost corner of the world. She knew better now than to imagine sun-tanning and sandy beaches for his 'by the sea'. More likely dismal skies, pale bad-tempered people shivering on the rocky shore.

'Your father works in Peterhead?'

'Aye, he does.'

She had grown up listening to the proper English of the BBC

World Service only to come to Britain and find people saying 'yes' like it was said back home in Arabic, *aye*.

'What does he do, your father?'

He looked surprised, his blue eyes surprised, 'Ma'dad's a joiner.'

Fareed hired people like that to work on the house. Ordered them about.

'And your mother?' she asked.

He paused a little, stirred sugar in his coffee with a plastic spoon. 'She's a lollipop lady.'

Shadia smirked into her coffee, took a sip.

'My father,' she said proudly, 'is a doctor, a specialist.' Her father was a gynaecologist. The woman who was his wife now had been one of his patients. Before that, Shadia's friends had teased her about her father's job, crude jokes that made her laugh. It was all so sordid now.

'And my mother,' she blew the truth up out of proportion, 'comes from a very big family. A ruling family. If you British hadn't colonized us, my mother would have been a princess now.'

'Ye walk like a princess,' he said.

What a gullible, silly boy! She wiped her forehead with her hand, said, 'You mean I am conceited and proud?'

'No, Ah didnae men that, no . . .' The packet of sugar he was tearing open tipped from his hand, its contents scattered over the table. 'Ah shit . . . sorry . . .' He tried to scoop up the sugar and knocked against his coffee mug, spilling a little on the table.

She took out a tissue from her bag, reached over and mopped up the stain. It was easy to pick up all the bits of sugar with the damp tissue.

'Thanks,' he mumbled and they were silent. The cafeteria was busy, full of the humming, buzzing sound of people talking to each other, trays and dishes. In Khartoum, she avoided beng alone with Fareed. She preferred it when they were with others; their families, their many mutual friends. If they were ever alone, she imagined that her mother or her sister was with them, could hear them, and spoke to Fareed with that audience in mind.

Bryan was speaking to her, saying something about rowing on the river Dee. He went rowing on the weekends, he belonged to a rowing club.

To make herself pleasing to people was a skill Shadia was trained in. It was not difficult to please people. Agree with them, never dominate the conversation, be economical with the truth. Now here was someone whom all these rules needn't apply to.

She said to him, 'The Nile is superior to the Dee. I saw your Dee, it is nothing, it is like a stream. There are two Niles, the Blue and the White, named after their colours. They come from the south, from two different places. They travel for miles over countries with different names, never knowing they will meet. I think they get tired of running alone, it is such a long way to the sea. They want to reach the sea so that they can rest, stop running. There is a bridge in Khartoum and under this bridge the two Niles meet and if you stand on the bridge and look down you can see the two waters mixing together.'

'Do ye get homesick?' he asked, and she felt tired now, all this talk of the river running to rest in the sea. She had never talked like that before. Luxury words, and the question he asked.

'Things I should miss I don't miss. Instead I miss things I didn't think I would miss. The *azan*, the Muslim call to prayer from the mosque. I don't know if you know about it. I miss that. At dawn it used to wake me up. I would hear *prayer is better than sleep* and just go back to sleep, I never got up to pray.' She looked down at her hands on the table. There was no relief in confessions, only his smile, young, and something like wonder in his eyes.

'We did Islam in school,' he said, 'Ah went on a trip to Mecca.' He opened out his palms on the table.

'What!'

'In a book.'

'Oh.'

The coffee was finished. They should go now. She should go to the library before the next lecture and photocopy previous exam papers. Asafa, full of helpful advice, had shown her where to find them.

'What is your religion?' she asked.

'Dunno, nothing I suppose.'

'That's terrible! That's really terrible!' Her voice was too loud, concerned.

His face went red again and he tapped his spoon against the empty mug.

Waive all politeness, make him dislike her. Badr had said, even before his windows got smashed, that here in the West they hate Islam. Standing up to go, she said flippantly, 'Why don't you become a Muslim then?'

He shrugged, 'Ah wouldnae mind travelling to Mecca. I was keen on that book.'

Her eyes filled with tears. They blurred his face when he stood up. In the West they hate Islam and he . . . She said, 'Thanks for the coffee,' and walked away, but he followed her.

'Shadiya, Shadiya,' he pronounced her name wrong, three syllables instead of two, 'there's this museum about Africa. I've never been before. If you'd care to go, tomorrow . . .'

No sleep for the guilty, no rest. She should have said no, I can't go, no I have too much catching up to do. No sleep for the guilty. The memories come from another continent.

Her father's new wife, happier than her mother, fewer worries. When Shadia visits she offers fruit in a glass bowl, icy oranges and guava, soothing in the heat. Shadia's father hadn't wanted a divorce, hadn't wanted to leave them, he wanted two wives not a divorce. But her mother had too much pride, she came from fading money, a family with a 'name'. Of the new wife her mother says, bitch, whore, the dregs of the earth, a nobody.

Tomorrow, she need not show up at the museum, even though she said that she would. She should have told Bryan she was engaged to be married, mentioned it casually. What did he expect of her? Europeans had different rules, reduced, abrupt customs. If Fareed knew about this . . . her secret thoughts like snakes . . . Perhaps she was like her father, a traitor. Her mother said that her father was devious. Sometimes Shadia was devious. With Fareed in the car, she would deliberately say, 'I need to stop at the grocer, we need things at home.' At the grocer he would pay for all her shopping and she would say, 'No, you shouldn't do that, no, you are too generous, you are embarrassing me.' With the money she saved, she would buy a blouse for her mother, nail varnish for her mother, a magazine, imported apples.

It was strange to leave her desk, lock her room and go out on a Saturday. In the hall the telephone rang. It was Fareed. If he knew where she was going now . . . Guilt was like a hard-boiled egg stuck in her chest. A large cold egg.

'Shadia, I want you to buy some of the fixtures for the bathrooms. Taps and towel hangers. I'm going to send you a list of what I want exactly and the money . . .'

'I can't, I can't.'

'What do you mean you can't? If you go into any large department store . . .'

'I can't, I wouldn't know where to put these things, how to send them.'

There was a rustle on the line and she could hear someone whispering, Fareed distracted a little. He would be at work this time in the day, glass bottles filling up with clear effervescent, the words 7Up written in English and Arabic, white against the dark green.

'You can get good things, things that aren't available here. Gold would be good. It would match . . .'

Gold. Gold toilet seats!

'People are going to burn in Hell for eating out of gold dishes, you want to sit on gold!'

He laughed. He was used to getting his own way, not easily threatened, 'Are you joking with me?'

'No.'

In a quieter voice, 'This call is costing . . .'

She knew, she knew. He shouldn't have let her go away. She was not coping with the whole thing, she was not handling the stress. Like the Nigerian student.

'Shadia, gold-coloured, not gold. It's smart.'

'Allah is going to punish us for this, it's not right . . .'

'Since when have you become so religious!'

Bryan was waiting for her on the steps of the museum, familiar-looking against the strange grey of the city, streets where cars had their head-lamps on in the middle of the afternoon. He wore a different shirt, a navy blue jacket. He said, not looking at her, 'Ah was beginning to think you wouldnae turn up.'

There was no entry fee to the museum, no attendant handing out tickets. Bryan and Shadia walked on soft, thick blue carpets that made Shadia want to take off her shoes. The first thing they saw was a Scottish man from Victorian times. He sat on a chair surrounded with possessions from Africa, over-flowing trunks, an ancient map strewn on the floor of the glass cabinet. All the light in the room which came from this and other glass cabinets, gleamed on the wax. Shadia turned away. There was was an ugliness in the lifelike wispiness of his hair, his determined expression, the way he sat. A hero who had gone away and come back, laden, ready to report.

Bryan began to conscientiously study every display cabinet, read the posters on the wall. She followed him around and thought that he was studious and careful, that was why he did so well in his degree. She watched the intent expression on his face as he looked at everything. For her the posters were an effort to read, the information difficult to take in. It had been so long since she had read anything outside the requirements of the course. But she persevered, saying the words to herself, moving her lips . . . *During the 18th and 19th centuries, north-east Scotland made a disproportionate impact on the world at large by contributing so many skilled and committed individuals. In serving an empire they gave and received, changed others and were themselves changed and often returned home with tangible reminders of their experiences.*

The tangible reminders were there to see, preserved in spite of the years. Her eyes skimmed over the disconnected objects, out of place and time. Iron and copper, little statues. Nothing here was of her, nothing belonged to her life at home, what she missed. Here was Europe's vision, the clichés about Africa; cold and old.

She had not expected the dim light and the hushed silence. Apart from Shadia and Bryan, there was only a man with a briefcase and a lady who took down notes, unless there were others out of sight on the second floor. Something electrical, the heating or the lights, gave out a humming sound like that of an air-conditioner. It made Shadia feel as if they were in an airplane without windows, detached from the world outside.

'He looks like you, don't you think?', she said to Bryan. They stood in front of a portrait of a soldier who died in the first year of this century. It was the colour of his eyes and his hair. But Bryan did not answer her, did not agree with her. He was preoccupied with reading the caption. When she looked at the portrait again, she saw that she was mistaken. That strength in the eyes, the purpose, was something Bryan didn't have. They had strong faith in those days long ago.

Biographies of explorers who were educated in Edinburgh; doctors, courage – they knew what to take to Africa: Christianity, commerce, civilization. They knew what they wanted to bring back; cotton watered by the Blue Nile, the Zambezi river. She walked after Bryan, felt his concentration, his interest in what was before him and thought, 'In a photograph we would not look nice together.'

She touched the glass of a cabinet showing papyrus rolls, copper pots. She pressed her forehead and nose against the cool glass. If she could enter the cabinet, she would not make a good exhibit. She wasn't right, she was too modern, too full of mathematics.

Only the carpet, its petroleum blue, pleased her. She had come to this museum expecting sunlight and photographs of the Nile, something to appease her homesickness, a comfort, a message. But the messages were not for her, not for anyone like her. A letter from West Africa, 1762, an employee to his employer in Scotland. An employee trading European goods for African curiosities. *It was great difficulty to make the natives understand my meaning, even by an interpreter, it being a thing so seldom asked of them, but they have all undertaken to bring something and laughed heartily at me and said, I was a good man to love their country so much . . .*

Love my country so much. She should not be here, there was nothing for her here. She wanted to see minarets, boats fragile on the Nile, people. People like her father. Times she had sat in the waiting room of his clinic, among pregnant women, the pain in her heart because she was going to see him in a few minutes. His room, the air-conditioner and the smell of his pipe, his white coat. When she hugged him, he smelled of Listerine Mouthwash. He could never remember how old she was, what she was studying – six daughters, how could he keep track. In his confusion, there was freedom for her, games to play, a lot of teasing. She visited his clinic in secret, telling lies to her mother. She loved him more than she loved her mother. Her mother who did everything for her, tidied her room, sewed her clothes from 'Burda' magazine. Shadia was twenty-five and her mother washed everything for her by hand, even her pants and bras.

'I know why they went away,' said Bryan, 'I understand why they travelled'. At last he was talking. She had not seen him intense before. He spoke in a low voice, 'They had to get away, to leave here . . .'

'To escape from the horrible weather . . .' She was making fun of him. She wanted to put him down. The imperialists who had humiliated her history were heroes in his eyes.

He looked at her. 'To escape . . .' he repeated.

'They went to benefit themselves,' she said, 'People go away because they benefit in some way . . .'

'I want to get away,' he said.

She remembered when he had opened his palms on the table and said, 'I went on a trip to Mecca.' There had been pride in his voice.

'I should have gone somewhere else for the course,' he went on, 'A new place, somewhere down south.'

He was on a plateau, not like her. She was punching and struggling for a piece of paper that would say she was awarded an MSc. from a British university. For him the course was a continuation.

'Come and see,' he said, and he held her arm. No one had touched her before, not since she had hugged her mother good-bye. Months now in this country and no one had touched her.

She pulled her arm away. She walked away, quickly up the stairs. Metal steps rattled under her feet. She ran up the stairs to the next floor. Guns, a row of guns aiming at her. They had been waiting to blow her away. Scottish arms of centuries ago, gunfire in service of the empire.

Silver muzzles, a dirty grey now. They must have shone pretty once, under a sun far away. If they blew her away now, where would she fly and fall? A window that looked out at the hostile sky. She shivered in spite of the wool she was wearing, layers of clothes. Hell is not only blazing fire; a part of it is freezing cold, torturous ice and snow. In Scotland's winter you live a glimpse of this unseen world, feel the breath of it in your bones.

There was a bench and she sat down. There was no one here on this floor. She was alone with sketches of jungle animals, words on the wall. A diplomat away from home, in Ethiopia in 1903, Asafa's country long before Asafa was born. *It is difficult to imagine anything more satisfactory or better worth taking part in than a lion drive. We rode back to camp feeling very well indeed. Archie was quite right when he said that this was the first time since we have started that we have really been in Africa – the real Africa of jungle inhabited only by game, and plains where herds of antelope meet your eye in every direction.*

'Shadiya, don't cry.' He still pronounced her name wrong because she had not shown him how to say it properly.

He sat next to her on the bench, the blur of his navy jacket blocking the guns, the wall-length pattern of antelope herds. She should explain that she cried easily, there was no need for the alarm on his face. His awkward voice, 'Why are you crying?'

he didn't know, he didn't understand. He was all wrong, not a substitute . . .

'They are telling you lies in this museum,' she said, 'Don't believe them. it's all wrong. It's not jungles and antelopes, it's people. We have things like computers and cars. We have 7Up in Africa and some people, a few people, have bathrooms with golden taps . . . I shouldn't be here with you. You shouldn't talk to me . . .'

He said, 'Museums change, I can change . . .'

He didn't know it was a steep path she had no strength for. He didn't understand. Many things, years and landscapes, gulfs. If she was strong she would have explained and not tired of explaining. She would have patiently taught him another language, letters curved like the epsilon and gamma he knew from mathematics. She would have shown him that words could be read from right to left. If she was not small in the museum, if she was really strong, she would have made his trip to Mecca real, not only in a book.

ALAN WARNER

Car Hung, Upside Down

The car hung, upside down high above the earth, in the leafless sycamore tree. Spunkhead was still strapped into his seat. Donald John had ended up kneeling on the squeezy black roof-padding. The loud, fast music kept playing.

Spunkhead, blond fringe hanging, his paleness flushed, reached out an inverted hand for the cassette eject button; then there was a roaring of blood in Spunkhead's ears, the sputtering hiss of upside-down-bust-radiator steam and another broke barrier fell away, past them from up on the hairpin above. Gatherings of naked winter twigs were violently twisted, shoved up against still-intact windscreen.

'Houston, we have a problem,' Spunkhead announced, his hair floating from side to side in space.

Donald John let out a yelp of laughter then went silent with a gulped breath. The roof he kneeled on was scattered with loose unmarked cassettes, empty beer bottles, sealed contraceptive foils, one or two pence pieces, cigarette butts and old *Playboy* and *Hustler* magazines. Some pages had flopped open.

'I wondered where that one had gone,' Donald John says quietly, moving out a hand to touch the girl on the shiny page.

'You okay?' Spunkhead let his arms dangle and placed both palms on the car roof.

'Watch it! Throw that seatbelt lock . . .'

'Aye. We get out. You first. The car gets lighter.'

'This is, we are agreed, a good thing?'

'Affirmative.'

'I'll get out first. Less weight in the car.'

'And the cradle *will* rock Donny ma man! Fuck, what if the whole kit and caboodle comes a-tumbling down?'

Donald John turned back from the door, creased his forehead at Spunkhead hanging there, then picked up a copy of *Hustler* that he rolled into a tube and slid down the front of his breeks. 'I snap a branch, I want her with me, all the way down, to break my fall.' Donald John cooried on the upside down car roof and used both hands to gingerly wind the window handle the wrongish way, as if he was stirring a real big, thick pot of porridge oats. He looked at the digital clock, fitted into the dash:

10:33

Spunkhead was thoughtful. 'Hoi, Donny. No think, when yon Macpherson, the sergeant, finally gets this car down, its gony be a bit of a brasser . . . it being full of scud mags, flunkies, beer bottles; you gave The Argonaut a hurl back from the dance Saturday night so there must be roach ends in your fucking ashtray here.' Upside down, Spunkhead yanked the ashtray further out: a fresh confetti-ing of tumbling ash sprinkled down, butts pattered on the back of Donald John's leather jacket.

'I'll destroy all evidence . . .' Donald John stopped winding the window. A few twigs had sprung in the gap the window had created. '. . . Turf some of this shite out then.' Donald John reached about him, gathering the magazines, bunching the metallic contraceptive packets in his fist, rolling the Beck's bottles nearer with his fingertips.

'Yup. *That's* it.' Spunkhead encouraged from above.

Donald John shoved the cassettes and coppers to one side, revolved the window handle more, then started thrusting out and away the porno mags, into the spriglets, till they flappered and turned, then each of the beer bottles went out. Spunkhead and Donald John could hear the green glass bottles bump the high, thick boughs and clash through the twig clusters downwards or leap out, then the painful longness of the bottles' freefall in open air, before they hit the heavily rooted ground without smashing. 'Must be what Richard bloody Branson does as yet another balloon plummets earthwards,' Donald John muttered.

Spunkhead's laugh sounded different upside down. More strained.

Donald John says, 'Ample roach-ends here – every fucking butt's a joint. Fucked if I got to smoke half of it either. Every cunt've had in this car must've been spliffing away.'

'Hey now Donny! Got to watch you don't get a three year ban. Like me! C'mon now, get a move on, so's I can get down from here. Funny isn't it? When you're a kid, you cant get enough of being upside down; all the bloody time youre aye doing handstands just to see what the world looks like the other way up . . . here, look at the steering wheel fucks sake!'

The normally top of the steering wheel, now the lower section, was bent over almost as far as the plastic covering on the dash speedo. Spunkhead's tone went serious. 'Donny. You have a seatbelt on, ya daft cunt?'

'No. But thats just my weight on the wheel. I'd my two arms stretched out and the top of the wheel just took my weight was all.' Donald John cupped the contraband butts in his hands, swung his arms out the window, and set the little scraps free, as if he was releasing a trapped bird. He changed the subject. 'You mind I don't unbalance this thing when I get out.'

'You're unbalanced enough.'

Donald John wound on up the window, though when the car was the correct way up, this would be called winding *down* the window. He started shoving his legs out through the bunch of twigs; angrily, he snapped a persistent, inward-shoving one – the buff bark strained pale green then cracked backwards, revealing the powder-white innards beamed with a green tubering, so bright in the air. His legs dangled in space; he had to lean back to wriggle outwards through the window, so his face lay close to Spunkhead's.

'Careful for fucksake,' Spunkhead says.

'Mmm.' Donald John caught the door moulding and swung his outside feet about, feeling for branch or bough. 'Fucking grab me if I cant get something here.'

He got the angle of a solid bough below him, where it joined into the main trunk. He grimaced as he let his canvas shoe take more weight and get squeezed into the branch's emerging angle. Donald John reached, got a grab where the twigs were thickening into a branch, shoogled to test, then shoved himself away from the car. He was out. He was stood, one foot canted up high on the jutting branch, the other foot wedged where the bough was moulded from the main green-barked trunk. Donald John edged his other leg down and this adjustment dropped his head to just below the dunted-up car roof. He smelled the smoke.

'Okay champion?' Spunkhead called. He held the roach to his hung-upside-down face and blew out a cloud. Holding the joint in his mouth, he sprung the seatbelt lock and walked backwards on his hands then fell softly, his legs curling him onto the roof. Spunkhead's face appeared in among the sprung-back twigs. 'Where'd my joint go? I dropped my joint there.' He crawled back around the roof, in frantic little circles that made the car creak and shift a bit. His face appeared again. 'I cannae find it.'

'Fucking get down here,' Donald John snapped. 'Watch it though. Hoor of a difficult getting balanced, but with having the extra height you should manage. If youre no too stoned. See, yon branch there – just use that springy one to tug out then, once your legs are secure here, heave over on that. I'll climb down to make room.'

Very gingerly, Donald John swivelled, trembling a little, stepping one canvas shoe over another, pushing his palms onto the cold wood trunk. He kneeled, placed an arm out behind him and lowered one foot to the next branch down. His leg jellied a bit . . . nervous . . . but he stretched out then got his arse down on the bough he'd been on. He slipped through the fanning of branches, arms locked secure behind so he could get those feet solid in that belowness there.

Meanwhile above, Spunkhead was wriggling from the car then placing his Nikes on wood near Donald John's left ear.

Donald John used this moment of pause in their onward, downward movement to a terrestrial base to take greater account of their surroundings.

The sycamore's upper boughs and reachings were almost as elevated as the broken barriers of the missed hairpin. Thinking back, Donald John could accept the tree as something of a landmark in the undulating lochside lands. The sycamore had always been there, in summer its lather of leaves shimmering before the waters of Loch Feochan by the raised beach. Up on the school bus, back when he was fifteen, you could see further down the tree than from a car on the hairpin. The cliff was sheer from the road. The fall from the verge to down there through the tree to all its roots, embedded in the earth . . . you would need to stop your vehicle, get out on that blind corner and peek down to see the muddied underside of the car. Donald John peered up in his imaginings, expecting some hesitant but concerned faces keeking downwards – their features hidden by chins compressed into chests – toes on the lip of the cliff.

There were no faces up there on the bluff above. As he was swallowing, looking skywards, Donald John heard the downgrading gears of a vehicle approaching the hairpin. He turned himself to survey beyond the main trunk and across the cultivated gowan fields to where the main road reached the waterside. The vehicle, a high-sided van, moved along round the trees, its white sides attracting the pinkish light. The van rounded the trees, its angular shape broken and divided up among the fat boughs, and it was gone.

Donald John now turned himself towards the raised beach and shoreline across the flat patchwork of fields. The redness of the morning was slicked on the loch surface. The actual stone beach, where land met water, out of sight, was concealed below the raised fields which ended in a puff of sand among some small dunes.

Donald John squinted at those little anchored boats, the factory ship with its trembly arc lights, brighter than anything, and then the shorecast bulk. Donald John says, 'Look,' then his eyes moved from the beaching out to the widening waters of the delta and open oceans. 'Look for fuck's sake.'

'Jesus Christ all fuckity, is that no a sight?' Spunkhead shook his head. 'That's fucking biz*arre*.'

From there, in their perch, they could see the grill-like grin ranged up the side where the cutting had begun. The tail's upper fin fallen hugely to one side, hung over in resignation.

'Lets get down there, Chavvy,' Spunkhead laughed, looking out onto the red sea loch, the low swell crests letting sunlight razor down their lengths. The same beauty of a shepherd's warning had been reflected in each oncoming windscreen Donald John had met on their homeward race before the hairpin, their trajectory to the tree, and the beginning of their descent . . .

Spunkhead was locked, spread-eagled among the boughs, twigs and branches a couple of steps up from Donald John. The looming of the upside-down car darkened his surroundings as Donald John began to climb to another bough, way down through the twig canopies.

'I'm fucking knackered,' Spunkhead piped up.

'Aye?' Donald John concentrated on getting a foot down.

'*Aye*. I need my seventeen or eighteen hours a night.'

Donald John looked up at the Spunkhead profile, then gazed out to the red-tinged loch. Donald John lifted a finger to his forehead, saw the thick sparkly sweat on the fingertip. He could feel the pinheads up in his hairline. He looked down – how the boughs grew thicker, lower in the tree.

Down at the next level Donald John looked back up to see Spunkhead stood on a thicker bough, leaned into the trunk, working into the bark with a Swiss army knife.

'Whatre you doing?'

'Carving my initials. Cant be all the way up here and not make ma mark.'

Donald John began to notice how all the porno mags seemed to have got snared up there in the clusters and branches, pages hung open and draped over branches, or splayed out on twigs so these naked, flesh-coloured little women seemed to sprout over the whole tree, sitting up in the branches like leopards, holding themselves open for the dumb stretches of farmland and the moss-strewn clutter of boulders and fence-posts below.

'The loch's so fucking red,' Donald John murmured, and more to himself than to Spunkhead. He could see the wee slivers of bright, creamy bark with green, tickering down from aboveness. He squinted up, knowing Spunker would carve also:

+

DEIRDRA

:Irish chick the both of them shagged in the toilets of the plane coming back from Alicante, her wee daughter was with her.

Donald John let out a smile, an awful long smile – a smile that took in the years – oh, the years, oh aye, so many years all gone. Donald John looked up at the car hung, upside down, then laughed then stopped, coughed.

'Whatre you getting off on, Chavvy?' Spunker muttered, concentrating.

Donald John wearily sat, fished the mag out of his Levis. He tried to read a story. It was an art form, how quick they got onto the boning. Some had perfected the introductory necessities to a single sentence:

> On Tuesday, the sexy, long-legged new assistant in the office said the photo of my husband on my desk really had her running to the toilet; so I said, 'Friday at 8, here's the address,' so on Friday my husband put his long tongue in her throbbing mouth as soon as she walked in; I lifted her skirt from behind and . . .

Aye. Donald John tossed the mag away forward and at least saw this one turn on itself, then the heavy-thumbed spine, splat the ground amongst the beer bottles of the earth.

Donald John began to slide lower. He went, pensively, 'Weird, aint it? I was talking to these townie lads when I was at the heliport in Eh-berdeen there, and the cunts were going on about the intra-caseys of how a lassie gets fucked by an Alsatian, or how she sucks a donkey's dick, or how about this scene where two chicks were getting a snake's head up them and that, yet these are the same pricks that every day call you and me fucking sheep shaggers. These twisted wanks watch so many porn movies they know the manual on animal intercourse . . . eh?'

Spunkhead blew onto his completed treetrunk carving. A little silence of satisfaction immediately followed.

'Know what I mean? I wouldnt know the first thing about how to get it on with a beast, but these cunts from the city are fucking experts! Even know what size of tea-chest you need to stand on to shag a horse up its ass.'

'Pervy town cunts,' tutted Spunkhead. 'When I was at primary, there was a cunt, Beamer McKechnie. Fat fuck. Says he found a sheep, drowned upside-down in a river pool with its sheep's fanny lips all open, like a chubby girls, so he fucked it.'

'Fucked a dead sheep?'

'Aye.'

'Ohh ya cunt ya.'

'I mind his big beaming happy fucking face the Monday morn. *Aye*. That fat cunt fucked the dead sheep okay.'

Donald John thought, then says, 'Walking back from the Turbines Bar, one nighty there, freezing as fuck; been on the drams all day. So fucking cold, the new loch had frozen solid. I'm stalking along the shore road, singing to myself, and I hear this scraping, this manic slide-sliding. It's way *out* there. Out in the dark on the ice flow. Well I'm scared, deep scared man; I can hear this living being, this animate life form, *out* there . . . moving. So I climb down the road embanking and I step onto the ice. Its so thick, I feel more solid on it that I do on the floor of my flat. I'm walking out there, walking through the night, on the solid deep-water ice. Below a star, towards this mad, circulary scratching. When I get close I'm scared – I can hear it snorting, breathing, knocking with its free hoof – cause its a stag, a big fucking deer with horns, back legs stuck solid into the ice, one front leg right deep into the solid ice. Mustve gone through the surface just before nightfall when it was thinner, then got all froze solid into it, as nightcold descended. I'm thinking to myself: if a big hoor of a stag can go through this ice so can I, and the bastard can see me, smell me too, so near, struggling on the ice. I just start tip-toeing back to the shore and I leave the bastard there.'

'So? You never shagged it then, you poof? Buggered it from behind while it was helpless?' says Spunkhead.

Donald John slowly looked upwards. 'Nay. But yon city cuntsdve been out gang-banging all fucking night, gang-bang on ice spectacular! The old Torvill and Dean.'

Donald John wiped more sweat offof his forehead and was about to restart his descent when he smelled it and looked up. Smoke was gushing out the open window of the car, hung upside down above them.

Donald John and Spunkhead stopped observing the morning and quickly began lowering themselves from branch to branch.

'We cannae do it. You and your fucking joints. We cannae make it. Drop's too far,' Donald John shouted.

'Here.' Spunkhead was quicker on the tree, he was right behind him, swinging off his jacket and dangling one leather arm down to Donald John's fingers.

A flame puffed out the open car window high above them, and then some burning thing fell down past. A swirl-trail of grey smoke was going off, turning over across the fields towards the red shoreline. Donald John knotted two arms of his own jacket and Spunker's together. There was a whoosh of combustion up there. Spunkhead giggled nervously above.

Donald John tied the arm of a joined-together-jacket round a bough and, as if he was a parachutist, tipped off the branch. He yelled in pain, the tied-together-jackets took the weight and swung him in the shore direction. Donald John let go, bicycled his legs in the air, hit, rolled on the hard earth. He stood up immediately and began striding towards the loch that was now lit up all white by the sun.

'Hey Chubber, wait!' Spunkhead was down.

But Donald John wasnt waiting. He was walking onwards, till he crossed the first fence, palms digging into the wired barbs, and he reached the lip of raised beach, where he saw the two gulliver ships from the marine laboratory at Dunbeg anchored offshore there, and saw the lilliput men around the slab-peeled blubber, saw the loch.

'No.'

Far behind, Spunkhead was calling. Then the guts of the burnt-out car began to crash down through the cindered syca- more, exploding in a column of orange sparks. Ahead lay the gassed-up bulk of the shored whale, its blunt snout up-shore near the dune-grass, the loch slicked red with blood from the stripped white, fleshed flanks. Blood the same colour as the black glut of bloods hupping into Donald John's back throat from his rib-ripped innards.

Donald John: unbelieving that his last minutes should only have had ridiculous concerns in his mind . . . his mind where he'd prepared so long, only to have this humiliating trash, jumble and mess up there. Unbelievable.

He'd fallen. Eyes close to the grass were dead. Maybe. Splendid morning reflected in the black pupils. Maybe not. The day only just started and dead!

Far across the fields, above the buzz of chainsaws' dull impacts on the whale, Spunkhead was running, screaming, first in this direction, then in that.

BIOGRAPHICAL NOTES

John Aberdein was born in 1946 and again in 1994 as Pan Doricist. In between times he was much influenced by his family, Nietzsche, Rilke, Beckett, Blake, MacDiarmid and the enormous diversity of folk who love and work or try to work in Scotland.

Leila Aboulela was born in 1964. She graduated from the University of Khartoum then studied statistics at the L.S.E. In 1990 she moved with her family to Aberdeen. Her work has appeared in a number of magazines and anthologies.

Alison Flett. Previously writing under the name Kermack, Alison now prefers to use Flett, a surname passed down through generations of daughters on her mother's side of the family.

Other publications include the Rebel Inc. booklet *Writing Like a Bastard*. Alison is still writing, though not so much like a bastard any more as she now spends most of her time having fun with her new daughter Aphra.

Janice Galloway has written four books: *The Trick is to Keep Breathing, Blood, Foreign Parts* and *Where You Find It*. The extract from *Foreign Parts* reprinted here was an early draft: the other is from a work in progress called *Mother*.

Shug Hanlan attended Bonnybridge Primary, Denny High School, Stevenson College, Edinburgh, the College of Marxist Education in Derbyshire, Newbattle Abbey College, Dalkeith, and the Universities of Canterbury, Miami and Glasgow. Where he learned to write is another matter entirely.

A number of the pieces printed here were first published in the magazine *Northwords*.

Brent Hodgson was born in New Zealand and grew up in great misery, his family having no knowledge of either the Rangers or the Celtic football teams. Since taking up the pen in Scotland his work has been published in literary magazines. None of his published fiction or poetry is required reading in the English Faculties of American Universities. The writer Pete Fortune of Dumfries maintains it is not required reading, anywhere. In 1995 he received a Scottish Arts Council Writers bursary.

Robert Alan Jamieson currently lives in Edinburgh. He has published three novels and a book of poems, *Shoormal* (1986). Since 1993 he has co-edited the journal *Edinburgh Review*.

James Kelman novelist and short-story writer; occasional playwright, essayist; based in Glasgow.

Gordon Legge was born in Falkirk, brought up in Grangemouth. To date, he's published three books: *The Shoe, In Between Talking About The Football,* and *I Love Me, Who Do You Love?* A fourth, *Near Neighbours*, will be published early next summer.

Duncan McLean was born in Aberdeenshire in 1964, spent ten years in and around Edinburgh and now lives in Orkney. He has written stories, novels, plays and a travel book: *Lone Star Swing: On the Trail of Bob Wills and his Texas Playboys.*

James Meek was born in England in 1962 and grew up in

Scotland. He lives in Russia. He wrote the novels *Drivetime* and *McFarlane Boils the Sea* and the story collection *Last Orders*.

Ali Smith was born in Inverness in 1962. Her book of short stories, *Free Love*, won the Saltire First Book of the Year award and a Scottish Arts Council Book Award. Her first novel, *Like*, was published by Virago this year.

Alan Warner was born and brought up in Oban. His first novel, *Morvern Callar*, won a Somerset Maugham award and has been filmed by the BBC. His second novel, *These Demented Lands* was published earlier this year.

Irvine Welsh has published four books: *Trainspotting* (1993), *The Acid House* (1994), *Marabou Stork Nightmares* (1995) and *Ecstasy* (1996).